WILDLIFE CROSSINGS OF HOPE

WILDLIFE CROSSINGS OF HOPE

CONNECTING CREATURES AROUND THE GLOBE

TEDDI LYNN CHICHESTER

ILLUSTRATED BY JAMIE GREEN

books for a
better
earth
™

holiday house • new york

A ***Books for a Better Earth***™ Title
The Books for a Better Earth™ collection is designed to inspire
young people to become active, knowledgeable participants in
caring for the planet they live on.
Focusing on solutions to climate change challenges and human
environmental impacts, the collection looks at how
scientists, activists, and young leaders are working
to safeguard Earth's future.

To my mother, Nadine Chichester, and in memory of my father,
Ben Chichester —TLC

Illustrator dedication TK

PROLOGUE
WILDLIFE ON THE MOVE

*H*OOFPRINTS, paw prints, a flash of fin in a surging river, or a glimmer of wings against a darkening sky: we don't want our own—our human—footprints to erase the signs of the marvelous creatures with whom we share this planet.

Let's explore together how scientists, engineers, environmentalists, and lots of everyday people are working to make sure that the wildlife so essential to Earth's health, vitality, diversity, and beauty can freely move through the landscapes, waterways, and skylines of this richly inhabited planet.

And let's find out how you, too, can help wildlife navigate a world that seems evermore crowded—with cities, roads, farms, shopping malls, and other human artifacts. All members of the animal kingdom—mammals, birds, fish, reptiles, amphibians, and insects—need our help. We, in turn, need them to survive and flourish, not simply for the resources or even the beauty they provide, but because they truly are our kin, our fellow passengers on an increasingly fragile planet. We travel together toward an uncertain future whose more hopeful outcomes you and I can help ensure—for ourselves and for the wild beings who have their own irreplaceable roles within a beautifully complex web of life.

However, as we will learn from conservation biologists, those scientists who closely study nature in order to protect it: to preserve the lives of individual creatures and of whole species, we must first make sure they have safe places to live *and* safe paths to travel as they search for food, water, mates, and maybe even a new home.

These paths can take the shape of specially designed bridges, but also large protected strips of land and even freely rushing rivers and streams, often newly liberated from the dams that once blocked the travel routes of fish and other aquatic species. As wilderness areas shrink and splinter, creating safe passages is the key to survival for wild creatures around the world.

CHAPTER 1
HOME RANGES AND RANGING BEYOND

LIBERTY CANYON:
A BIODIVERSITY HOTSPOT

On a warm Southern California morning, I stand on a mountain slope fragrant with sage and spiky with dry chaparral. A lizard scampers under a nearby rock, and a red-tailed hawk hang glides in the breeze. Just over the ridge behind me lies the Pacific Ocean. I gaze across at the golden-brown hills to the north, then down to an incongruous sight: ten lanes of pavement, an eight-lane freeway running along a two-lane access road, the former thick with traffic whizzing through the canyon in both directions.

This formidable roadway, U.S. Route 101, extends from Washington State down to Southern California, where it divides the Liberty Canyon Natural Preserve. Not far from Los Angeles,

Liberty Canyon and its surrounding areas are part of what ecologists call a **biodiversity hotspot**, one of only thirty-six such regions in the world. These hotspots are rich in extraordinary flora (plants) and fauna (animals) that are direly threatened by human disturbance, which can include housing, infrastructure (like roads, railways, and airports), croplands, and climate change.

So although the traffic itself is but one of many dangers to wildlife, the 101 Freeway decisively divides a vital dwelling place whose creatures need to move freely from place to place—as one extraordinary animal named P-22 made dramatically clear to Los Angelinos and, eventually, the world.

In 2012, a young male carnivore made an incredibly perilous journey. From his birthplace somewhere in the Santa Monica Mountains, the coastal range that slopes down into Liberty Canyon, to Griffith Park in the heart of Los Angeles, he traveled east at least 7 miles (11 kilometers). And, miraculously, he made it across two of California's busiest freeways, the 101 and the 405. He also faced other hazards we can only imagine.

Scanning Griffith Park remote-camera photos one day, wildlife biologist Miguel Ordeñana was shocked to discover the unmistakable image of a mountain lion, also called a cougar or puma, the region's most charismatic, and most threatened, species. As the news of this sighting got out, followed by stunning photos, local residents were captivated by the beauty and bravery of P-22 (the twenty-second puma in a National Park Service study)—and by the unlikelihood of such a wild creature camping out in the United States' second most populous city.

So, as those living near Hollywood tend to do, they made him an international celebrity. They also embraced him as the handsome mascot for a remarkable, and remarkably ambitious, project: a massive bridge across the 101 Freeway right here in Liberty Canyon that will soon help mountain lions and other native fauna find safe passage—and one another.

P-22's story reminds us that wild animals of all shapes and sizes live and move among us, even in a bustling metropolis like Los Angeles. His odyssey also prompted his countless fans to wonder: Why did he leave the mountain stronghold of his birth? And what can we do to help make such excursions safer for all wild creatures, many of whom don't navigate the human landscape as expertly as P-22?

We'll return to Liberty Canyon and to the tale of P-22, but let's first explore the concept of **ecology** where scientists study nature's intricate webs of life.

THE WOVEN WORLD

Whether a magnificent polar bear or a homely stag beetle—or an adventurous SoCal cougar—all creatures are part of a whole intricately connected community. Here plants, fungi, animals, and abiotic elements—nonliving features such as terrain, water, and weather patterns—work together to create a complex, interdependent network known as an **ecosystem**.

If you've ever stood next to—or climbed—a sturdy oak tree, you've been immersed in a compact though utterly vibrant ecosystem. Basking in the sun's rays, the oak leaves convert light to energy and nutrients through a process called photosynthesis. In the meantime, networks of underground fungi

strike up a mutually beneficial, or symbiotic, relationship with the oak via its root tissues, allowing the two organisms to nourish each other. Rain and groundwater bathe the tree's branches and roots in life-giving moisture, while caterpillars and other insects feast on its leaves (and perhaps one another!). And busy squirrels forage for protein-rich acorns, which end up as a tasty meal or a buried seed that may one day spring forth as a new oak tree. This sapling would, in turn, become its own dynamic new ecosystem, an essential part of an even larger community of plants, animals, and abiotic features called an oak woodland. These processes and relationships form the beating heart of the natural world.

The ecosystems of biodiversity hotspots like Liberty Canyon are especially rich in native and even endemic species. **Native** or **indigenous**, as opposed to exotic or invasive, means that the species has developed over a very long time within a specific region. An **endemic** plant or animal can be found nowhere else on earth. For scientists, these endangered hotspots offer wonderful opportunities for learning—and for deepening our commitment to protecting the ecosystems we rely on and are part of.

The root of the term ecosystem, and of ecology is the Greek word "oikos", which means "home." It is this home, this habitat, with all its crucial resources—food, water, and shelter—that wildlife conservationists around the world are working very hard to protect.

To save an imperiled creature, they tell us, we must first save its home.

THERE'S NO PLACE LIKE HOME: WILDLIFE HABITATS

If home is at the core of ecology, we need a much more expansive definition of "dwelling" than we're used to when we consider wildlife **habitats**. For us, home may be a small two-bedroom apartment, a rambling ranch-style house, or a down-town condo. And animals–again, a term encompassing birds, mammals (like us!), fish, reptiles, amphibians, and insects–have their specific shelters: burrows, dens, nests, streambeds, and lodges.

Wildlife habitats, though, both include and stretch beyond such shelters. A northern spotted owl builds her nest in a tree hollow or broken treetop, but she spends much of her time roosting on redwood branches and swooping through the understory of the coastal rainforest in search of wood rats and other favorite prey. This whole tract of woods–home base in the nest, nearby roost, and as many as 8,400 acres (3,400 hect-ares) of lush old-growth forest–is her habitat.

When wildlife biologists speak of habitats, they often refer to **home ranges**, a term that perfectly captures the blend of staying put and moving around that defines the life of a wild creature. While a beaver living in rural Michigan may rest, hide from predators, or care for young in her lodge, she must also venture out to find food and fell trees for the dams she builds. Her home range must be large enough, with enough plants to eat, freshwater streams to remodel, and trees to harvest, to sustain her, her family, and others of her kind.

Wide-ranging animals like grizzlies and gazelles (and the northern spotted owl) require expansive habitats with lots of

room to roam. And creatures compelled to find a new home, as well as those who embark on the often epic excursions of seasonal migration, remind us that wildlife habitats encompass an ever-shifting array of homes and home ranges. As all types of wildlife journeys become more difficult in the wake of disappearing wilderness, experts and activists are putting the concept of "landscape connectivity" front and center.

CONNECTIVITY AND THE MOTIVES FOR MOVEMENT

While many of us think of connectivity in terms of how easily our laptop can pick up the boba shop Wi-Fi or how quickly we can message our friends via cell phone, ecologists measure **connectivity** as the degree to which wildlife can move between and within suitable habitats.

Wild creatures need wild places. A creature's ability to roam around its home range is crucial to its survival, and protecting its individual habitat is critical. Yet natural or undisturbed landscapes are quickly disappearing, or becoming isolated in what scientists call **habitat patches** or **habitat fragments.** These small, disconnected pieces of land, usually carved out by human activity, strand and divide populations of wildlife. Unless we find ways to enlarge and connect scattered patches, such fragmentation may spell doom for many species who need to move more freely within their original home ranges—or away from them, either permanently or seasonally, during migration.

Imagine a koala in a rural part of eastern Australia. He's happily munching on eucalyptus leaves, the staple of his diet.

One day, a crew with chainsaws and bulldozers and excavators clears out a large chunk of his forest. Eventually pavement is laid down, and cars, tractors, and trucks begin traversing his territory, his home range. Well, now connectivity between stands of eucalyptus is lost. The koala's once-intact (undisturbed) home range is now two separate, dramatically divided fragments, either of which may be too small to sustain the local population, or specific community, of koalas.

This kind of habitat disruption and destruction is happening all across globe, threatening countless species, in large part by impeding wildlife mobility—an agile lynx chasing down a snowshoe hare in northern Canada, a herd of bison roaming an Oklahoma prairie, a family of ring-tailed lemurs swinging between trees in the Madagascar rainforest. All of these animals need to move in order to hunt, forage, find mates, and evade danger, whether naturally occurring or, too often, created by us.

Wanting to help the koala continue his within-home-range movements, his daily commute or routine search for food, water, and shelter, conservationists and government officials might build a **wildlife crossing structure**. This would go over or under the road and allow him to travel between separate strips of habitat. Wide overpasses clothed in greenery, narrow passages tunneling beneath highways, and even rope bridges for tree-dwelling creatures to swing along: these are all specially built structures that offer crucial lifelines to animals as they encounter the countless roads, often thick with traffic, that thread through the land. In fact, Australia has a number of these wildlife bridges, and those who monitor them have learned that shy koalas much prefer dark tunnels to highly exposed overpasses!

Yet ecologists and environmental activists envision, and are fighting for, a kind of connectivity that goes beyond, in scope and ambition, even the grandest of wildlife bridges. **Wildlife movement corridors**, also called **greenways** or **wildlinks,** are extensive swaths of protected land, and even water, that link crucial habitat fragments. These corridors have become the best hope for threatened and endangered species—hemmed in, cut off, marooned—and for biodiversity itself.

Connectivity becomes even more critical when wild creatures need to venture far from their homes. Thousands of species, including nearly half of all birds, migrate every year, taking seasonal journeys to and from their breeding grounds.

The migration route of the western spadefoot toad, indigenous to Baja and western California, is among the shortest in the world. Spending most of the year in upland grassy terrain, this stout little amphibian travels during the rainy season a mere 43 yards (about 40 meters, or half a football field) down to small pools of rainwater. Here it will breed, then make the short trek home, where it will settle back into its underground burrow.

The Arctic tern, on the other hand, is quite the world traveler. In fact, this hardy seabird takes the longest migratory journey of any creature, flying each year from its breeding grounds in the northern tip of the globe down to Antarctica, and then back again. Arctic terns accumulate lots of frequent-flier points for this 50,000-mile (80,467-kilometer) round trip!

As they leave their original home ranges, migratory creatures often face a true gauntlet of human-made obstacles.

When connective links between habitats are severed, creatures on the move face much harder journeys, including another kind of expedition called dispersal.

Dispersal involves individual creatures or even whole local populations relocating to a new habitat, often some distance from their original home. It is young creatures in search of their own territories, say an Alaskan moose or a timber wolf in Wyoming, that most often disperse (like young adults going away to college!). Yet a forest fire or housing development might evict a whole community of chipmunks or desert kit foxes that then must find a new place to live.

CLIMATE-WISE CONNECTIVITY

The search for food and water and shelter, the need to reproduce, the flight from predators, the encroachment of *homo sapiens*. Joining these key catalysts that keep wildlife on the move is **climate change**, dramatic shifts in weather patterns around the world, resulting in large part from the burning of fossil fuels such as petroleum and coal. Many people in particularly vulnerable regions are tragically displaced from their homes by forest fires, floods, and coastal inundation (due to sea level rise)—all stemming from or at least exacerbated by climate change.

Animals, too, are becoming climate refugees. If their habitats aren't directly destroyed by increasingly frequent (un)natural disasters, extreme drought and other dangerous symptoms of global warming—another term for climate change—are pushing wildlife toward cooler regions: poleward and into higher elevations.

Scientists and others who want to help climate-stressed creatures connect to new sites of safe, resource-rich habitat must not only understand where animals now live and roam but also project where new atmospheric conditions will propel them. As they strive to create climate-wise connectivity, wildlife experts like Nature Conservancy ecologist Dr. Mark Anderson use computer modeling as well as good old-fashioned fieldwork. For the former, scientists may create computer-generated maps that identify "climate-resilient" habitats and track wildlife movement within and between them. They may also feed data into software programs that can simulate and even predict, for example, weather patterns in West Africa, or track migratory routes of birds and land animals that pass through there. On the other hand, when a biologist is slogging through a Florida swamp to observe alligators lurking among the cattails, she is performing fieldwork.

Wildlife-movement maps overlaid with climate data are among the key tools that allow scientists to discover and protect climate-resilient locations for the crossing structures and larger corridors that wild creatures need as they move through a dramatically warming planet.

While ecologists like Dr. Anderson study where animals are going as they search for new homes, other scientists explore the plight of creatures left behind, isolated in ever-dwindling patches of wilderness. We'll now turn to the unfolding crisis of habitat fragmentation, which underscores just how urgently wildlife needs permanent, extensive, and truly welcoming corridors of hope.

CHAPTER 2
THE PROBLEM WITH PATCHES

When we consider the habitats of wild creatures, we may imagine vast emerald green forests—dim, quiet, far away from city, suburb, or farm. But more and more, our world is encroaching on theirs, turning once-natural dwelling places—desert, rainforest, or grassland—into island-like outposts surrounded by an ocean of man-made structures or land cleared for crops and cattle. Throughout the globe, creatures are confronting a bewildering array of buildings and airports and shopping malls and fences and roads.

This is the turbulent world that encircles many animals, stranding them on separate habitat patches. These fragments of land have become small and isolated—no way in, no way out. The smaller and farther apart these patches become, the harder it is for wildlife to travel for food or mates or shelter—and even to survive.

Connectivity, their critical lifeline, has been broken. Too soon, a patch of land may become a forest of ghosts and memories of what once was.

SCENES OF EVOLUTION, THREATS OF EXTINCTION

This modern-day story of entrapped, vanishing wildlife is part of an ongoing saga with **extinction**, the death of entire species, at its center. But in order to understand extinction, we need to grasp another key concept: **evolution**. This involves eons-long processes of change and adaptation—an organism's precise attunement to particular conditions in a particular place.

In 1835, the British naturalist Charles Darwin visited a string of tiny islands off the coast of Ecuador as part of an epic voyage of scientific discovery. He encountered an astonishing variety of flora and fauna on the Galápagos Islands, including giant tortoises and exquisite songbirds. Closely examining differently shaped and sized tortoise shells and finches' beaks, Darwin began to see that life on Earth didn't just magically (or divinely) appear. Instead, it developed, changed, *evolved* over time and in response to place. Creatures and plants adapted to their environments, gaining and losing physical and behavioral traits in a process called "natural selection." Thus, a species found its precise "niche" within its world—both a physical place and an ecological role.

Ponder, for example, the western spadefoot toad, whose very name bespeaks her precise adaptation to her arid habitat. Her shovel-like appendage allows her to burrow into even very hard ground, and thus to escape the hot sun, as well as the coyotes and crows who would like to make her their lunch. This adaptation took millions of years to perfect, and when a species goes extinct, its whole evolutionary heritage, both genetic and ecological, disappears as well.

When we contemplate extinction, we may think of long-departed creatures, like the lumbering dinosaurs that loom out of the misty past like storybook monsters. Yet today's headlines also provide obituaries for nature's most recent losses.

Scientists warn that half of the world's species face extinction by 2050, and point to such anthropogenic, or human-caused, factors as air, water, and soil pollution, as well as climate change. But it is habitat destruction and fragmentation that wildlife biologists decry as the often-overlooked drivers of extinction. Fortunately, many biologists, botanists, and climate scientists are working in the relatively new field of fragmentology. These scientists are helping us understand why wild creatures need much more than small, isolated pockets of land.

THE LARGEST LABORATORY IN THE WORLD

In 1979, an American tropical biologist named Dr. Thomas Lovejoy launched what has been called "the most important ecological experiment ever done," the Biological Dynamics of Forest Fragments Project (BDFFP). In this study, scientists track what's happening within habitat patches created by the ongoing **deforestation**, or destruction of huge tracts of trees, within the Amazon rainforest.

Learning that the Brazilian government required landowners near the northern city of Manaus to conserve half of their rainforest property, Dr. Lovejoy hatched a brilliant plan. He convinced ranchers and government officials to let him and his colleagues shape the protected portions into what we might call, paradoxically, intact fragments. Scientists from around the world could then study these forest patches. The project has united biologists, ornithologists (who study birds), entomologists (insects), primatologists (primates), and many others.

Now "the world's largest and longest-running experimental study of habitat fragmentation," the BDFFP has been unfolding for over forty years. The project contains eleven patches, or reserves, ranging from 1 to 100 hundred hectares (roughly two and a half football fields for the smallest and, for the largest, two Disneylands). Among other things, the project serves as a laboratory where scientists can observe in real time the grim process of ecosystem decay: how ecosystems break down.

Dr. Lovejoy and his colleagues soon discovered that size really matters when it comes to wildlife habitats. Initially in the smallest, but later even in the roomier reserves, scientists saw how overcrowding led to fierce competition for space and food. Soon, whole communities of creatures began disappearing in a process called **local extinction**. This stage serves as a warning sign of larger **regional extinction**, which in the worst-case scenario becomes **absolute** or **global extinction**, the irreversible collapse of an entire species.

In those patches that did sustain some wildlife, only the more common, resilient species remained. These hardy survivors are called **generalists**, who can adapt to even the most disturbed, crowded environments. But the Amazon, like other biodiversity hotspots such as the one in Liberty Canyon, has long nurtured **specialist species**, creatures with very strict habitat and dietary needs. If their home disappears, they can't simply pack up and move on; they will vanish as well.

Watching local extinction unfold, scientists learned that what surrounds the patches and what happens at their borders definitely matter just as much as their size.

EDGES AND THE MATRIX

As far too many species in the BDFFP disappeared, Dr. Lovejoy and his colleagues focused on two key concepts central to understanding habitat fragmentation: edge effects and the matrix.

Just like an actual island can be encircled by a raging sea or a quiet lake, so, too, are wildlife habitat patches surrounded by very different environments. Imagine one island in the midst of storm-tossed ocean and another gently lapped by the waters of a lake. Which one would you rather travel to in your canoe—or embark from for a nice swim? Animals face the same kind of dilemma as they move between habitat fragments.

What surrounds the habitat patch or fragment is called its **matrix** (plural, matrices). Matrices can be hostile (difficult or impossible for wildlife to cross, like a highway) or permeable (relatively open to travel, like an orchard or ranch).

This brings us to the concept of **edge effects**, the conditions at the border between the habitat patch and the matrix—in the case of the BDFFP, the *deforested* matrix. If these conditions are too harsh, wildlife inside the habitat patch may avoid leaving and instead retreat farther inside the "island" sanctuary. No escape route and less space to roam: survival seems more precarious than ever. Here is where the dangerous impacts of climate change on habitat become especially clear.

Wildlife in the Brazilian Amazon has evolved in the wet, shady recesses of the rainforest. So for these creatures, the most destructive edge effects include conditions like light, heat, wind, and dryness. Rapidly heating and drying the planet, climate change pushes creatures like shade-loving butterflies and moisture-dependent amphibians away from hot and dry habitat edges and even farther into the cool but already crowded interior—and closer toward local extinction.

We'll now meet a vital member of the Amazonian eco-community who has indeed suffered local extinction within the BDFFP, but who is making a big difference elsewhere in the Amazon. Its absence from smaller forest fragments underscores just how much is lost when ecosystems begin to unravel and animals have no corridors to connect them to more promising habitats.

WHITE-LIPPED PECCARIES AND AMAZONIAN TREE FROGS: A DYNAMIC DUO

While Kermit and Miss Piggy may be the most famous amphibian-porcine pair you know, another such odd couple has played a starring role in the ongoing story of the BDFFP. Not long after the ranchers felled and torched the land for cattle, a very different stocky ungulate, or hoofed mammal, took its final bow in the reserves. This highly endangered indigenous creature nurtures and even beneficially shapes its ecosystem, creating homes where other smaller members of a biologically diverse forest can thrive.

Resembling a wild boar and weighing about 88 pounds

(40 kilograms), the white-lipped peccary—all thick-necked, hunched bravado—sports a bristly dark coat and signature white markings around its flat round snout.

As the world's foremost peccary expert and champion, Dr. Harald Beck, tells me, "Of course, everybody loves a strong tiger or a cute panda, but a peccary is really for special people! It makes amazing sounds (pounding hooves, clicking teeth), lives in huge, friendly groups called squadrons, and makes a distinct, strong smell that creates a kind of peccary internet for territory marking and social messaging—all this, and it can easily outrun you."

Despite their sturdy build, white-lipped peccaries fall into the category of specialist species, creatures with very particular needs. Namely, access to huge amounts of food and land to roam. White-lipped peccaries are also edge averse and "highly reluctant to enter clearings"—the scorched-earth matrix surrounding the patches. Thus, these hulking beasts of the Amazon rapidly vanished from all the BDFFP fragments.

If white-lipped peccaries have special needs, they also do special things. To cool off or get rid of pesky parasites, peccaries roll around in the mud, creating depressions called wallows. These wallows fill with water and invite even more, well, wallowing, which, in turn, widens and deepens these peccary-built ponds. Wallows also attract other creatures, such as giant water bugs (aka toe-biters!), which become permanent residents. Bats and ocelots may stop by for a quick drink. Thus Dr. Beck and other tropical biologists call peccaries **ecosystem engineers** that shape their forest world in wonderfully enriching ways.

Yet another group of more diminutive creatures shares the stage with the swaggering peccary. They have evolved and adapted to their rainforest home in equally impressive ways. Like the white-lipped peccary, rainforest tree frogs represent essential **indicator species**: creatures that signal the change to "health (or decay)" of entire ecosystems—ecosystems that may have become, like the BDFFP patches, disconnected from the wider wilderness's vital streams of life.

As the most important beneficiaries of their rowdy neighbors' engineering expertise, several colorful rainforest tree frogs rely almost exclusively on peccary wallows to breed. During mating season, both male and female frogs descend from their arboreal homes, gripping the trees with suction-cup-like toe pads, yet another product of evolutionary fine-tuning. When they find a peccary wallow to their liking, the amphibian couple builds a leaf nest just above its rim. Eight to ten days later, newly hatched tadpoles splash down, grateful tenants of peccary-designed digs, until they climb onto land with freshly sprouted legs in a couple of months.

Working as an amphibian researcher in the BDFFP, Dr. Barbara Zimmerman observed two related and, in her words, "rather spectacular" *Phyllomedusa* tree frogs that disappeared from the reserves almost immediately after the white-lipped peccaries suffered local extinction. The giant monkey frog and tiger-striped leaf frog both need peccary wallows for breeding, and Dr. Zimmerman explains why: "These species have evolved mechanisms to keep their eggs and tadpoles away from predation by fish—hence their requirement for ponds that are not connected to streams or rivers." Yet even these ingenious adaptations offer no protection if the rainforest continues to splinter and shrink, vanquishing these Amazonian amphibians and the squadrons of ecosystem engineers they rely on.

Together, this unusual but perfectly matched pair reminds us that extinction, even in its preview stage as a local vanishing, permanently erases key strands, literal DNA strands, of nature's legacy.

BDFFP SCIENTISTS: FRAGMENTOLOGISTS AND CONSERVATIONISTS

As they witness such losses, BDFFP researchers, who usually spend part of the year at the site, are by no means just observers. Along with creating the Biological Dynamics of Forest Fragments Project in Brazil, Dr. Tom Lovejoy has also worked tirelessly with the region's local people to sustain both rainforest biodiversity and Indigenous culture, a culture that is itself deeply immersed in and protective of the natural world. In Dr. Lovejoy's work, fragmentology exposes the fault lines that crack the land into pieces, while conservation helps heal the rifts, restoring and reconnecting the forest, for the animals and for the people.

All those who work in the reserves are passionate defenders of the natural world, helping create (or restore) wildlife connectivity throughout the world, as Dr. Lovejoy's closest collaborator, Dr. William Laurance, does with his foundation, ALERT. By fighting new roads in Ecuadorian rainforests, as well as deforestation in China and Guyana, Dr. Laurance's Alliance of Leading Environmental Researchers & Thinkers is safeguarding the habitats and travel routes of wildlife around the globe, including in Brazil and throughout the Amazon Basin.

And BDFFP scientists are even seeing filaments of connection unfurl in the project site itself. Although today, neither white-lipped peccaries, giant monkey frogs, nor tiger-striped leaf frogs have returned to their original home grounds in the project site, BDFFP researchers are seeing some heartening signs. Secondary forest (succeeding the old-growth, primary forest) has sprung up around a few of the reserves. These new forests are becoming passages that allow at least some wildlife to move back into the larger fragments.

Just eight years after the BDFFP was launched, conservation biologist Dr. Jay Malcolm was "stunned one day to find capuchin monkeys way out in the middle of the secondary forest." This new growth provides a crucial pathway for creatures most sensitive to fragmentation, like capuchins and bare-tailed wooly opossums, which Dr. Malcolm and his colleagues also discovered in the now-more-sheltering matrix.

STITCHING THE WORLD BACK TOGETHER

In the mathematics of ecology, to divide is to subtract. As the still-unfolding Biological Dynamics of Forest Fragments Project underscores, when deforestation and other forms of habitat loss separate populations of wild creatures, their numbers inevitably plunge.

Created to quell the tide of extinction, the Endangered Species Act (ESA), signed into U.S. Law in 1973, recognizes that we need to protect not just the creatures themselves, but also their homes and "the ecosystems upon which endangered species and threatened species depend." Thankfully, then, various "critical habitat" zones gain protection as more species are declared threatened or, the most urgent status, endangered. More recently, both the America the Beautiful Initiative launched in 2022 by President Joseph Biden, and a pledge that same year by 196 countries at the United Nations annual biodiversity summit (COP15) are tackling the extinction crisis in the spirit of the ESA, with ambitious plans to conserve vital wildlife habitat, often within designated parks and refuges.

Nature reserves, sanctuaries, national parks: all of these offer some safety, some version of *oikos*, or home, to the creatures with whom we share this planet. Yet these protected patches are still just that: pieces of a wider world.

Wildlife movement corridors, even mini versions like those now linking some of the Amazon rainforest fragments to one another and to the larger old-growth landscape, are providing lifelines to creatures all over the world, creatures otherwise stranded on islands of *our* own making.

As roadways in particular continue to devour and fragment the land, creating often deadly barriers for creatures on the move, remarkable wildlife crossings, crucial components of corridor networks large and small, are springing up across the globe. We'll now see how architects, engineers, and transportation officials have been joining ecologists and wildlife conservationists to build a variety of crossing projects that are burrowing beneath and reaching over highways, saving countless wild creatures, and helping repair the tattered wilderness.

CHAPTER 3
NAVIGATING ROADS OF DANGER

A pair of pikas climbs a steep rock walkway. A grizzly bear lumbers across a sturdy log. Swinging through the jungle canopy, a baboon grasps outstretched branches linking the tallest trees. A rainbow trout rides the rapids of a free-flowing river. A herd of water buffalo plunges through a ravine carved out by last year's rain. A king snake wends its way through an abandoned prairie dog tunnel.

As it so often does, nature here shows us the way as we seek to restore harmony and, yes, connectivity to the world, a world that, as we've seen, has split asunder into a jumble of fragments. For all of these traveling creatures, the land, trees, water flows, and even fellow wildlife have fashioned an intricate, inviting transportation system that the animals expertly traverse.

THE ROAD BEST NOT TAKEN

Infinitely harder for them to navigate is the vast network of roads that crisscross—and slice through—the earth. An astonishing 40 million miles (over 64 million kilometers) of paved and unpaved roads encircle the planet, gobbling up needed hab-itat, blocking vital pathways, and, too often, leaving unlucky creatures lifeless, or gravely injured on the side of the road.

Even a chain-link fence or cement-lined irrigation canal can stop a creature from getting where it needs to go. Scien-tists call these blockages **barrier effects**. But a busy freeway like the one snaking through Liberty Canyon is the most literal and most dangerous kind of roadblock that wild creatures face. Wildlife road mortality, roadkill, wildlife vehicle colli-sions (WVC): all ugly expressions for an even uglier reality that threatens the survival of animals throughout the world, including many already endangered species.

Over a million terrestrial vertebrates, animals with a back-bone, lose their lives on the road each day in the U.S. alone. That's one every 11.5 seconds! The fact that traffic kills more than eight million birds every year just in Brazil reminds us that aerial (as opposed to terrestrial, or earthbound) species are by no means immune from the carnage. Harder to imagine are the estimated 228 *trillion* insects, those foundational eco-system members, killed by traffic each year throughout the globe.

When we turn to our own species, we learn that auto repair costs and hospital bills stemming from wildlife vehicle collisions total over eight billion dollars a year in the United States. More-over, each year in the U.S. over four hundred people die and several thousand others are injured in these terrible accidents. So when we seek to rescue our fellow creatures from harm's way, we are also protecting ourselves—our property and even our very lives.

Bridging the gap between transportation officials and conservationists are the people working in the relatively new field of **road ecology**. Scrutinizing wildlife migration routes, road-kill statistics, topography, and roadside vegetation, these scientists study the quite literal intersection between ecosystems and (human-made) transportation systems. They also team up with wildlife experts, engineers, and landscape architects to plan, design, build, and monitor the lifesaving crossing structures that get animals safely across rural roadways, interstate highways, and even colossal expressways and autobahns.

Besides investigating how roadways fragment the landscape and sever habitat communities, road ecologists point to what they call the **road-effect zone**, an area far beyond the pavement itself. Just as the scientists in the BDFFP study the edge effects of Amazon Forest fragments, where the heat, light, wind, and dryness of the adjacent clearings penetrate far into the reserves' patches, road ecologists analyze *and* work to reduce the ways that roads edge into and damage neighboring ecosystems, including wildlife habitats.

The road effects in these travel zones, similar to edge effects, include noise generated first by construction equipment and then by the traffic roaring down the completed highway. Roads are often repaired or widened, bringing even more bulldozers and asphalt mixers within earshot. Besides pushing wildlife, from large mammals to petite arachnids, farther back into already shrinking habitats, this frightening "acoustic interference" prevents creatures from hearing predators or prey, and from communicating with one another.

This is an especially crucial problem during courtship.

Scientists studying forest birds in Thailand blamed their declining numbers near a busy highway largely on traffic noise, "which distracts birds, making them more vulnerable to predation, and disrupts the singing for pairing during the breeding season."

Add to these sonic disturbances streaming headlights, vehicle fumes and vibrations, stirred-up dust, and the particulate matter (microscopic particles of solids and liquids) released from those tire shreds you often see littering the highway. You can imagine how road-effect zones might feel like battle zones to wild creatures! Even streetlights, which we welcome as beacons of safety, may in fact assault wildlife with "blasts of white LED light" shooting from giant lampposts, as Chicago-based landscape architect Robert Rock puts it.

Imagining the lives of these creatures, what they see and hear and how and where they move, is just what the remarkable people who conceptualize and create wildlife crossings do each day. Often with a multitude of species in mind, these engineers, biologists, designers, transit experts, and road ecologists must work together, across agencies and disciplines, to create buffer zones and bridges.

And they must consider questions like: What sites will best provide connectivity for creatures inhabiting all strands of the ecological web? Should we build what's called a "dedicated structure," made especially for wildlife use? Or instead **retrofit**, which means to redesign and modify, an already existing one? How do we get wildlife to use crossing structures? Should we build these linkages under, over, or even far above the road? It's these pressing issues that we'll turn to next.

PREPARING THE GROUND: BEHIND THE SCENES WITH CROSSING SPECIALISTS

Before a crossing project is "shovel ready," a fascinating, and years-long, planning process must take place. **Green bridges**, spanning highways with foliage-covered decks; **culverts**, and other types of underpasses, tunneling under roads; **arboreal** or **canopy bridges,** stretching from tree to tree high above the pavement: these are all part of the connectivity puzzles that we need to solve as we protect individual creatures and species and safeguard our planet's precious biodiversity. And as Associate Director of The Nature Conservancy's Climate Program Cara Lacey emphasizes, the ideal of connectivity—along with cooperation and compromise—must also unite those who envision, design, and construct wildlife bridges. Lacey tells me that, for example, officials from California's Department of Transportation work enthusiastically with biologists from environmental groups. In fact, Caltrans now has its own biologists on staff and is, in Lacey's words, truly "championing wildlife crossings."

It's a shared concern for imperiled wildlife that is building such seemingly unlikely partnerships. Conservation activists and engineers, road ecologists and landscape architects, professional scientists and students of all ages are forming their own rich ecosystems: webs of knowledge, passion, and empathy. These folks are, in turn, creating a vital network of wildlife crossings around the world.

As wildlife experts, transportation officials, road ecologists, and representatives from nonprofits gather together, let's listen in on a planning session for a series of crossings over and under a particularly deadly stretch of freeway in Southern California. The meeting opens with several crucial questions: How might an existing underpass be retrofitted to welcome wildlife? What impressive feats of engineering and fundraising could install an expensive overpass at a critical bottleneck or "pinch point," where a too-narrow wildlife travel route funnels animals toward the highway? How do we reconcile the needs of an astonishing array of species, from mountain lions to Timema walking sticks, deep-green night-foraging insects?

Years of wildlife surveys—using motion-triggered camera trap footage, radio collar monitoring, and roadkill statistics—have revealed several promising locales for the structures. Now it's time for wildlife experts to lobby for particular "suites" of animals: the invertebrates, small animals, birds, and medium to large animals that often require pretty different features in a crossing structure.

A bat expert describes the kinds of crevices that coastal pallid bats would need for roosting in a culvert. Speaking up for our friend the western spadefoot toad, one scientist suggests small ponds for the proposed overpass. Gray squirrels and big-eared wood rats would need rocks and dense vegetation for cover and forage. A carnivore specialist tells how some mountain lions "bounce"—warily approach and suddenly retreat—when they encounter a dark underpass. Perhaps a gentle light in the tunnel? Or maybe they would prefer an overpass?

All agree that each structure, whether tunneling under or sweeping over this busy thoroughfare, would need protected land—corridors—on either side. Native plants nearby to entice and nourish, fencing to keep creatures out of traffic and moving toward the crossing, and effective noise and light mitigation: these are also essential. As road ecologist Dr. Fraser Shilling suggests during the session, "dark and quiet paths" can invite, calm, and shelter even the wariest creature threading its way through our shared world.

Another consensus-building point comes from conservation ecologist Dr. Megan Jennings, who urges everyone "to think of crossings from the perspective of a range of species." Interspecies empathy, imaginative vision, and rigorous science flow through the meeting, one of several that will convene before the crossings project at hand becomes a reality. This congregation of devoted wildlife supporters move nimbly and cooperatively between the connectivity needs of one specific creature—bat, beetle, or bobcat—and the wider view of the whole ecosystem. We can also see crossing structures themselves—culvert, overpass, canopy link—as critical focal points in a broader pattern of eco-connections, corridors of hope that wild creatures can travel with soaring wings, thundering hooves, sturdy paws, slithering bellies, and minuscule insect feet.

CHAPTER 4
RECONNECTING WILDLIFE: UNDERPASSES, OVERCROSSINGS, AND CANOPY BRIDGES

In the midst of a citrus grove in Southern China, a miniature walkway, no bigger than an inch wide and made of dried bamboo, stretches between two trees almost ready for harvest. An orderly column of weaver ants flows along this tiny bridge, heading for their hunting grounds on a heavily laden mandarin orange tree. Mealy bugs and caterpillars will provide a tasty snack.

For thousands of years, citrus farmers in Guandong and Guangxi have been practicing a very special kind of organic farming, where ants, not toxic chemicals, control agricultural pests. Even today, farmers in this region build bamboo bridges for their weaver ant partners, who gobble up the bugs that would otherwise ravage the orchard.

While weaver ants balance on suspended bridges like tiny tightrope walkers, leaf-cutting ants in Costa Rica traverse a complex, ground-level trail system that includes bridges created by fallen branches and exposed tree roots. These clever insects have discovered that smooth wood surfaces allow for faster, easier travel than slogging through dense leaf litter. For an ant who may be hauling twenty times its own body weight in freshly harvested leaves, these elegant boardwalks provide welcome relief.

These tiny creatures, and the micro-pathways they traverse, lead us toward a vast array of specially designed wildlife bridges keeping animals safe from treacherous roadways throughout the globe. We'll first travel to several relatively small-scale structures before visiting a few truly ambitious crossing projects, including jumbo-size bridges and an amazing network of crossings that provides connectivity throughout a world-famous national park.

DOWN UNDER: CULVERTS, TUNNELS, AND AN ELEPHANT-SIZE UNDERPASS
A Hidden Passageway in the Redwoods

Tucked away in Northern California's Prairie Creek Redwoods State Park, where the world's tallest trees sip the fog from the nearby Pacific Ocean, you can find a cozy culvert, a squarish tunnel tucked beneath the Newton B. Drury Scenic Parkway just at the point where it crosses the creek itself. Now, most of the crossings we'll explore are, in fact, off-limits to people, and for good reason. Our presence can discourage animals from actually using these structures. But this culvert is simply part of the park's trail system. It can give us a sense of why an animal on the move might duck into it rather than brave the road.

When I first encountered this culvert as a very young girl, it seemed cavernous, dark, and musty, and a bit frightening. On a recent camping trip, I found it cozy and enchanting, with its foliage-draped entrances, moss-covered walls, and singing stream. I spoke with State Park Interpreter Kyle Achziger, who told me that many of the park's nonhuman inhabitants do indeed make their way through this compact passage, where a concrete ledge allows raccoons, possums, and chipmunks to scamper above the creek, which sometimes carries salmon along their own aquatic journeys. The damp earth next to the stream invites banana slugs, the bright-yellow symbols of the coast redwood forest, as well as the occasional Pacific giant salamander, another moisture-loving indigenous species. Cool, damp, quiet, and dim but not too dark, this passageway beneath the road seems a perfect, even *natural* crossing site for critters on the move—critters that want to avoid the traffic just above them.

As we watched a pair of young Roosevelt elk spar in a nearby meadow, I asked Achziger if elk ever use the culvert, but he told me that they simply stride boldly across the pavement. I guess these redwood royals know that they rule the forest, and that large yellow signs with handsomely antlered black silhouettes periodically advertise their roadside presence. Fortunately, the Newton B. Drury Parkway is not an enormous freeway, but a narrow avenue where sightseers adopt a leisurely speed.

Although I like to imagine banana slugs as the special guests of the Prairie Creek culvert, some wildlife crossing do, in fact, serve specific **target species**. These often threatened or endangered creatures receive particular attention—focused, long-term monitoring and interventions that will help protect them. Scientists, and superfans of the creatures we'll now meet, decided to intervene by helping them across the road.

Salamander Tunnels in Massachusetts

If giant salamanders on the go just happen to discover the Prairie Creek culvert, on the other side of the country, amphibian-loving residents in Amherst, Massachusetts actually *guide* thousands of native spotted salamanders toward two specially built tunnels beneath a busy road–the first wildlife crossings in North America constructed specifically for amphibians.

Each year, the swarming salamanders migrate from upland habitat to vernal breeding pools on the other side of Henry Street. (You might recall the western spadefoot toad's similar annual journey in Southern California, though he usually has no cars to contend with!) Until 1987, the first night of spring rain in this New England town brought not just wandering salamanders, but also a bucket brigade of adults and children, who stopped cars, scooped up the amphibians, and carried them across the street. Now "Big Night" requires fewer crossing guards, as two tunnels, each approximately 28 feet (8.5 meters) long, protect the creatures from the mass squashings that used to mark the occasion.

Made from repurposed airport runway drains and flanked by "drift fences" that help steer the salamanders to the openings, the Henry Street tunnel system attests to the community's compassion for their sleek nocturnal neighbors. The system also showcases the ingenuity of its designers, who included tunnel-top slots so rainwater from above can keep the moisture-loving migrators happy. For the Henry Street spotted salamader crew, *maintenance* and *monitoring* join *siting* and *building* as watchwords for successful crossing structures.

While Big Night remains the main event for the shiny black

creatures with yellow-and-orange spots, their human stewards, including children from neighborhood schools, work year-round to keep the fences in good repair and the tunnels free of debris. As they join together to protect these beloved amphibians, biologists and local volunteers continue to monitor salamander behavior during those rainy spring evenings. Observers note, for example, any "balking" (recall the mountain lions who "bounced" at the mouth of a scary underpass!). If needed, the tunnels are modified to make them more inviting for the Amherst amphibians as they go forth into their Big Night.

Mountain Marsupials Cross the Road in Australia

We'll now head to the actual Down Under to visit a pair of crossings that carries a pocket-size furry creature with an outsize tail beneath the road to safety. Like the Amherst salamander tunnels, the two small conduits running beneath the Great Alpine Road in southeastern Australia were specially built for a tiny target species—in this case, the critically endangered mountain pygmy possum, endemic to a fairly small mountainous region.

Though their numbers have dropped alarmingly in the past decades (to around two thousand in the wild), these huge-eyed, mouse-like creatures are remarkably hardy. They dwell in rocky highland terrain, where deep winter snows send them into hibernation seven months a year (pygmy possums are Australia's only hibernating marsupial).

Along with habitat fragmentation inflicted by roadbuilding and a popular ski resort, climate change, with its increasing droughts and heat waves so perilous for cold-adapted species, has brought these exquisite little possums to the very brink of extinction. In fact, scientists once thought that the mountain pygmy possum had actually passed into history! But in 1966 three small populations were found. Conservation biologists, together with Zoos Victoria and other dedicated organizations, are working hard to ensure that the story of this miraculous "resurrection" has a permanent happy ending.

Just as the spotted salamanders travel under Henry Street in order to breed, the pygmy possums of Mount Little Higginbotham embark on an annual migration that was for many years disturbed by a major highway. Female possums dwell year-round in the uplands, separated from their mates except during breeding season. When the male marsupials headed up the mountain to visit the females, the Great Alpine Road blocked their path, and their chances of siring a new generation.

Thankfully, two small concrete box culverts, about 52 feet (16 meters) long and adjoined to inviting rock-lined corridors, now allow the mini marsupials to reach mates in higher mountain slopes. These "tunnels of love" bring hope for one of the world's most threatened mammals. Though Australia's mountain pygmy possums still have some pretty steep slopes to climb before they're out of danger, monitoring methods such as population surveys and camera traps—those embedded devices that reveal the secret world of wildlife—show that these tunnels are indeed bringing this heroically resilient, and irresistibly cute, creature back from the edge once again.

Beneath the Highway in Kenya

While fragile bamboo bridges can support immense armies of

ants and slender tunnels shelter pygmy possums or salamanders on the go, the folks of Mount Kenya in East Africa would need a much larger, and sturdier, solution for a very special neighbor needing safe passage. Surprisingly, though, the world's largest land animal would not need a mammoth-size bridge.

Since time immemorial, the bush elephants of this region have been trekking between lowland savannahs and the forests of Mount Kenya, Africa's second highest peak. Farms, fences, roads—the familiar drivers of fragmentation—have increasingly blocked this now-endangered creature's home range movements and migratory journeys, as well as separated two local herds. And, as it does throughout the globe, climate change has made things even harder, heating up and drying out low-country habitat and making upslope trips to the cooler mountain forests with their plentiful forage even more necessary.

In instances of what's known as human-wildlife conflict, Mount Kenya's hungry, thirsty, hemmed-in elephants began to get in trouble with local people, trampling fences and raiding crops and water troughs. Concern for the animals and alarm about such behavior finally culminated in an ambitious plan to create a major wildlife corridor that would reopen the ancient pachyderm pathway and reunite the two herds.

The Kenya Forest Service (and nonprofits like the Mount Kenya Trust and the Lewa Wildlife Conservancy) worked with residents for several years to create the Mount Kenya Elephant Corridor. Yet the busy Nanyuki-Meru A2 Highway remained a stubborn barrier. A crossing structure was clearly needed, but would these massive creatures, the world's largest land

animal, actually enter a tunnel? (An underpass was, in this case, the most affordable option.)

Generous donors chipped in $330,000, and a 39-foot-long (12 meters), 15-foot-high (4.6 meters) tunnel was completed in December 2010. Its 19.7-foot (6 meters) width, the recommended minimum for culverts, may have seemed like a tight squeeze for the enormous creatures. And when East Africa's first elephant underpass opened, uncertainty lingered. Yet the very first night, a dauntless young bull elephant named Tony sauntered right in, and a few days later he led two other bulls from his herd through the passage.

Now thousands of elephants a year march safely below the highway, often in families and captured on camera. The lengthy corridor itself, with a strong assist from the underpass, has reunited the two Mount Kenya herds and given them a critical lifeline between their forested upland and savannah habitats below. Tony the pioneering pachyderm continues to use the undercrossing—though, like a few other bulls, he gets into mischief as well. Tony sometimes breaks farm fences, as Susie Weeks, Executive Officer of the Mount Kenya Trust, ruefully reports, adding, "The elephant family groups don't take these kinds of risks and are much more law abiding!"

With their own corridor and crossing structure, the project's target animals, Mount Kenya's elephants, truly have become an **umbrella species**, creatures who travel broad ranges and whose survival needs mesh with those of many other species. Thus the protections gained by an umbrella species—and its habitat—will, in turn, shield a whole community of other creatures. Now the elephants are sharing their underpass with other Kenyan wildlife, including African wild dogs, lions, chee-tahs, and leopards, as well as the occasional warthog and porcupine. Moreover, anti-poaching patrols guard the cru-cial corridor, protecting zebras, rhinos, and other vulnerable wildlife, along with the elephants themselves. And this region's intricate mosaic of farms, grasslands, and mountain forests—and now a world-famous underpass—has become a peaceful coexistence zone for native animals and human inhabitants. At least when Tony and other young delinquents aren't stirring up trouble!

OVER AND ABOVE: WILDLIFE OVERPASSES AND CANOPY BRIDGES
Building a Butterfly Bridge in Southern California

We'll now turn to overpasses, also called green bridges, **vegetated bridges**, and (in Europe) **ecoduct**s. These are less common than culverts and tunnels, which may already exist under roadways and can be modified for wild travelers. They're also often quite a bit larger than the tunnels and culverts we've toured. Yet for a tiny butterfly facing extinction in Southern California, scientists and transportation experts decided that over, rather than under, the highway would offer the Quino checkerspot butterfly the best route to recovery.

A gorgeous orange, black, and white round-winged jewel, the Quino checkerspot may be the only butterfly in the world to get its own expressway. An industrious pollinator of native plants, this species traces an unusually low flight pattern that brings it right into the path of speeding cars. Vehicle colli-sions, habitat loss, and climate-change-induced droughts that radically reduce needed water and forage landed the checker-spot on the Endangered Species List in 1997.

As members of the Riverside County Transportation Commission pondered extending a multilane thoroughfare in the city of Murrietta, they voted to include in their design and budget a wildlife crossing that could rescue these important ecosystem members.

Completed in 2018, the Clinton Keith Road overpass is doing just that, and though the Quino checkerspot is the project's target species, a rich variety of other creatures accompanies these endangered butterflies across rather than *into* traffic lanes. Deer and coyotes, California ground squirrels, Southern Pacific rattlesnakes and racers (another serpent), and an elusive Virginia opossum have all traversed the bridge. While they haven't yet made the journey across, endemic Stephens' kangaroo rats, with their charmingly alert expressions and spring-loaded legs, have shown up on camera foraging on the bridge. As she flutters out of harm's way, the featherweight Quino checkerspot butterfly, with the help of her own over-crossing, is also lifting her fellow chaparral species out of peril.

The Path of the Pronghorn Meets a Wyoming Highway

While butterflies float over traffic in Southern California, thundering hooves race across a series of structures, including two sagebrush-lined green bridges, built in the grasslands of the American West for the iconic pronghorn. With a white-striped neck and graceful horns that curve toward each other like an incompletely sketched heart, this flashy ungulate is the western hemisphere's fastest land mammal, clocking up to 60 miles (97 kilometers) per hour.

It's also an intrepid long-distance trekker. As these hooved wonders annually migrate through Wyoming from their winter range to summer feeding grounds, the ancient Path of the Pronghorn carries them through a grueling gauntlet (as long as 220 miles, or 355 kilometers, just one way) of both natural and man-made obstacles. In 2008, a large section of this route became the U.S.'s first federally-protected wildlife corridor.

One notorious roadway used to see countless pronghorn-vehicle collisions. But now Highway 191 at Trapper's Point no longer stops the stream of brown-and-white "prairie antelope" as they head for greener pastures. Wildlife "exclusion fencing" keeps pronghorns and other creatures such as elk and mule deer off the highway, and "funneling fences" guide them to the bridges themselves. In the face of too many road-killed and injured pronghorn, the Wyoming Game and Fish Department, lawmakers, transportation officials, scientists, nonprofit organizations, and individual pronghorn fans showed inspiring unity as they raised awareness and $11 million for the crossings project (over- and underpasses and fencing).

Biologists speculate that the pronghorn may have developed its incredible speed over millions of years as it was pursued by an even speedier sprinter: the now-extinct American cheetah. Yet until it could race *above* the path of traffic, the fleet pronghorn was no match for the man-made machines that too often cut short the journeys of wild creatures as they migrate, disperse, or simply try to cross the road in search of a meal or some good company.

A Forested Bridge for Brazil's Golden Lion Tamarins

Now let's do a quick stopover in Brazil, where a fluorescently bright pint-size primate faces extinction. The relentless deforestation that biologists in the BDFPP have been studying, and combating, for decades continues 2,784 miles (4,480 kilometers) southeast from Dr. Tom Lovejoy's project. Here, near the capital city of Rio de Janeiro, a rural four-lane highway plows through the Amazon home of the golden lion tamarin. Weighing barely a pound (0.5 kilograms) and living in just a few isolated patches of coastal forest, the critically endangered golden lion tamarin now has its own overpass connecting two critical habitats.

Lush with lowland Atlantic Forest shrubs and saplings, the bridge curves elegantly over the road and into dense forest on the north and pastureland on the south. A slim corridor of young trees threads through the pasture, connecting the bridge to vital protected habitat beyond: the Poço das Antas Biological Reserve. As Dr. James M. Dietz from Save the Golden Lion Tamarin (known in Brazil as AMLD) tells me, the group fought for years to get the local highway agency to build the structure, completed in 2020. But "completed" isn't quite the right word here. Vegetated overpasses—as their name reminds us—rely on nature's processes and timetable.

As Dr. Dietz explains, this structure is, in fact, a **forested wildlife bridge**, planted with a variety of native tree seedlings that will "provide continuous canopy over time," the kind of unbroken network of branches the imperiled golden lion tamarins need to get from place to place. According to Dr. Dietz, it will be a few more years before the trees are interlaced enough for the tiny arboreal monkeys to swing through. In the meantime, crab-eating foxes, bats, and armadillos are making use of the crossing. While the case of the golden lion tamarin overpass highlights the urgency of wildlife crossing projects, these highly social, communicative primates are finding their way forward, through forest corridors, large swaths of connective vegetation that the Association is preserving and planting, even as the tamarins await their turn to traverse their own bridge to a safer future.

Swinging Across the Road with India's Lion-Tailed Macaques

The last stop on our tour of wildlife overcrossings takes us not just over but high *above* the roadway. Large "troops" of the highly vocal lion-tailed macaques, an endemic primate listed as endangered, roam the ever-shrinking, fragmented rainforest of the Western Ghats, a vast mountain range that runs along the west coast of India.

This range is a major biodiversity hotspot where roads, along with tea plantations and sugarcane fields, have become the main drivers of habitat fragmentation. As in the Amazon Basin, deforestation in this region has broken many of the canopy connections that tree-dwelling creatures rely on. So lion-tailed macaques have had to drop to the ground in order to cross roads, where too often they lose their lives. As their habitats and food supplies disappear, this highly intelligent, immensely charismatic creature has been reduced to begging for food from tourists, and even breaking into houses, where they raid kitchens.

Dr. Joseph J. Erinjery, a zoologist who has been observing and advocating for these "kings of the top canopies" for many years, identifies the lion-tailed macaque as one of this mountainous region's key umbrella species. To bring these monarchs of the treetops back up where they belong, the Nature Conservation Foundation, a wildlife organization based in India, installed seven canvas canopy bridges in the Western Ghats's Valparai Plateau. A relatively new innovation, **canopy bridges** are usually made of rubber-coated canvas and rope or wood and resemble a ship's ladder. These inexpensive sky bridges fasten to trees on each side of the road and allow tree dwellers like primates, possums, and even porcupines to cross in high style.

The Valparai macaques didn't get just their own canopy bridges. Speed bumps, slow-down signs, and even two full-time "watchers" who act as lion-tailed macaque crossing guards and ambassadors/educators are part of the protection package. And, as Dr. Erinjery informs me, these measures are working.

Most of the resident lion-tailed macaques are using the bridges and far fewer of those who do descend to the ground are getting hit. Roadside begging from very persuasive primates is also down thanks to the watchers, who sternly warn drivers against handing out unhealthy snacks! Quoting one of the guards patrolling for speeders and junk food providers, journalist Trisha Gupta suggests just why these creatures inspire such loyalty and affection: "Sometimes they come and touch us gently on the shoulder. They're soft-type animals. If you don't disturb them, they don't disturb you."

PAW PRINTS AND DEER SELFIES IN A SOUTHERN CALIFORNIA UNDERPASS: AN UP-CLOSE LOOK

If Mount Kenya has its rambling elephant herds and the Hollywood Hills their international celebrity mountain lion, Puente Hills Preserve, several miles southeast of Griffith Park, boasts its own wild feline star. When gracing the Preserve with his presence, ZEK the bobcat ranges a roomy landscape: 4,000 acres (1,619 hectares) of oak groves and flowering buckwheat that's nestled amid freeways, subdivisions, and mini-malls.

As traffic increased on Harbor Boulevard, a major Southern California thoroughfare, ZEK and his bobcat cousins found their range shrinking and their lives threatened when they tried to ford the endless stream of cars. Just as P-22 became the poster cat for what will be the world's largest green bridge, ZEK helped inspire Los Angeles County's first dedicated wildlife underpass. And like all the best critter crossings, this cavernous tunnel, completed in 2006 for $1.4 million, links protected open space on each side of the road, 4,600 acres (1,862 hectares) to the west and, to the east, an impressive 14,000 acres (5,666 hectares). Stretching 160 feet (49 meters) beneath the road, comparable to the length of the overpasses we've just viewed, the structure is four times longer than Tony the elephant's much cozier culvert.

One sunny August morning, Michelle Mariscal, ecologist with the Puente Hills Habitat Preservation Authority, meets me just inside the Preserve. Mariscal knows these hills as well as anyone: grassland for burrowing spadefoot toads, hardy chaparral where coyotes stalk their prey, and coastal sage scrub,

perfect nesting grounds for one of the the region's most threatened most threatened birds, the coastal California gnatcatcher.

Studying, restoring, and protecting the ecosystem: add to
Mariscal's enviable job description the one "duty" (she clearly
doesn't see it as such) that brings me to the park today. Every
week or so, she visits the underpass to retrieve the SD (secure
digital) card from the trail camera and to investigate footprints.
Since people aren't allowed in the crossing, she hopes to see
only paw and hoof marks!

We climb into Mariscal's truck and head out of the tranquil
Preserve, entering Harbor Boulevard and a completely different world—of buildings, power lines, and noise. In a few min-
utes, Mariscal pulls over near a brushy hillside. We've arrived
at the underpass, but I never would have known it was there.
And that's just how Mariscal and her fellow scientists want it.
We scramble down a steep ravine, and there it is: a large, cor-
rugated metal tube, plugged into the road's concrete foundation and surrounded by dry foliage (it's summer in SoCal, after
all). A commemorative plaque doubles as a stern Keep-Out
sign, both warning and educating would-be trespassers that
human scent can deter wildlife.

As Mariscal opens the thick lock on the camera trap
installed at the entrance, she gives me the go-ahead for a quick
walk inside. The highly insulated structure keeps out traffic
noise, so I hear only the soft crunch of my hiking boots on the
sandy ground. The tunnel feels both spacious and secure, and
I imagine the soft pads of a slinky bobcat or the spiky feet of a
greater roadrunner, another native species, pressing into the
earth. The far side of the tunnel opens into a vista that includes

oil wells, concrete walls, houses, and those ubiquitous power lines. Yet I can see a clear path through a deep, vegetated arroyo that animals can follow. This arroyo, or gully, is a segment of the Puente-Chino Hills Wildlife Corridor that regained wholeness with the completion of the underpass.

When I return to the entrance, Mariscal kneels down to show me some prints. Deer, bobcat, coyote, none of which I could have identified without her keen eye. Thankfully, no boots or tennis shoes! Just before we go—we don't stay long in a place not meant for us—Mariscal secures the camera. So sensitive that even butterflies can trigger it, this device captures ten thousand images a week that she and a whole army of volunteers comb through. Handsome ZEK and other bobcats, I learn, have shown up on film a number of times, confirming that the underpass is connecting members of this keystone carnivore species with one another and with needed habitat.

On the drive back to the Preserve parking lot, Mariscal and I talk about how, more and more, wildlife are forced into smaller spaces, living near and even in disturbed landscapes such as those encircling the Preserve. Yet we also both find hope in people's willingness to set aside land just for wild creatures, like the coyotes and cactus wrens, skunks and gopher snakes that make their home in the Puente Hills Preserve, and that commute through the Harbor Boulevard Wildlife Underpass.

When I get home, I pore over a sampling of camera trap snapshots that Mariscal has emailed me. A coyote pup with outsize ears gazes soulfully into the lens. A mother mule deer and her fawn nibble on the grass edging the tunnel entrance. A bobcat (not ZEK, as this one isn't wearing a radio collar) poses confidently, her spotted coat and dignified profile creating a striking portrait. Clearly this roomy underpass in the heart of ultra-developed Southern California feels like a real refuge for them. They're not hurrying through, but lingering, taking a breath and a maybe bite to eat—sheltered from the traffic above, free to continue on their own travels, when they're good and ready.

As we continue our tour of vegetated bridges and secluded tunnels, we'll travel to some truly ambitious crossing projects to get a closer look at how an incredibly varied group of species is making its way across and under urban expressways and rural roads. And we'll check in on the historic Liberty Canyon project, which promises to link two struggling populations of mountain lions, patiently awaiting their bridge to a brighter future, and to one another.

CHAPTER 5
SAFE PASSAGE FOR BIODIVERSE TRAVELERS: LARGE-SCALE WILDLIFE CROSSINGS

*E*xcept for the Prairie Creek culvert and the Puente Hills underpass, each of the crossings we've just visited serves a particular target species: salamanders slipping under rain-slick streets, pronghorn flashing over prairie highways, lion-tailed macaques navigating an arboreal superhighway. Other wild residents and migrants are welcome to enter, provided they can fit—or, in the case of canopy bridges, swing!

Diverse communities of creatures rather than one high-profile species inspired the bridges and underpasses we'll now explore. And these crossings are, on the whole, much larger than the structures we've already seen. In fact, we could call a few of these mega-bridges, including, of course, the massive Liberty Canyon crossing. We'll also tour the world's largest *system* of crossings, a vast network of culverts and overpasses that keeps grizzlies and geese, boreal toads and bobcats moving safely through a ruggedly beautiful landscape.

CRAWLING, HOPPING, AND GLIDING UNDER AUSTRALIA'S CALDER FREEWAY

While Australia's Mount Higginbotham possum crossings (try saying that three times!) were custom-built for petite marsupials, a much larger underpass in Australia serves a diverse group of wildlife, from tiny brown toadlets to strapping eastern gray kangaroos and stocky wombats. We've arrived in the small town of Macedon, about a four-hour drive from pygmy possum country.

Here a road upgrade project threatened to divide two crucial sections of the Black Forest, a wildlife-rich habitat for such fantastically named creatures as the sugar glider, the Victorian smooth froglet, the kookaburra, and the superb fairy-wren.

Well, in 1997, the expanded Calder Freeway did, in fact, sever a pretty big chunk of forest. But something unusual and promising accompanied this construction project: $3 million (in Australian dollars) for a wildlife crossing, set aside by the agency in charge, VicRoads (Victorian Government Roads Corporation). Fortunately, governments around the globe are finally keeping nature in mind as they build and enlarge infrastructure (recall the Quino checkerspot butterfly bridge). But in 1997, awareness of habitat fragmentation's terrible toll and the funds to restore connectivity were both in very short supply. In this respect, when construction crews arrived at the site, the Slaty Creek Wildlife Underpass was truly groundbreaking, both figuratively and literally.

Flooded with natural light, the 230-foot-wide (70 meters) structure features a welcoming open-span design. The road above, resting on 39-foot-high pillars (12 meters), is split into two segments, between which mature eucalyptus trees invite arboreal creatures such as koalas, brushtail possums, and southern brown tree frogs. Rich vegetation that sweeps into the structure creates crucial connectivity to the forest itself, beckoning foragers and shade seekers.

An eclectic assemblage of "faunal furniture," acquired not at the mall but from nature's own storehouse, includes logs, rocks, stumps, branches, and brush piles that offer cover to shy visitors like garden skinks, and even habitat if they decide to move in permanently, as many reptiles and amphibians do. A number of native birds and twelve species of bat have found the structure expansive enough to fly through and secure enough to roost in.

A series of wooden glider poles provides yet another kind of crossing structure. These poles serve as surrogate trees for sugar, ringtail, and squirrel gliders, who prefer to remain aloft even as they pass under the freeway. Like flying squirrels, these nectar-loving marsupials open their arms, spread their superhero-cape-like membranes and float gracefully from tree to tree, or pole to pole, avoiding the ground below and the road above.

How do we know so much about what goes on in the Slaty Creek Wildlife Underpass? Shortly after its completion, a graduate student in Environmental Management named Rodney Abson spent twelve months monitoring the structure, recording animal sounds, studying footprints, analyzing scat (wildlife droppings), and discreetly observing as wombats waddled into, kangaroos bounded through, and scarlet robins hung out in this haven under the highway. Most encouragingly, Abson discovered that nearly all of the 116 species of fauna dwelling in the Black Forest region were actually using the crossing!

Other young people, too, studied the underpass and played important roles as **citizen scientists**, nonprofessionals who collaborate in person or online with biologists and other researchers, helping them understand particular species and ecosystems. Students from the Macedon Primary School helped create an artistic and educational exhibit teaching local residents about the treasures in their very midst: the Slaty Creek crossing itself and the wonderful variety of wildlife that lives in the Black Forest. These creatures can now move more freely within their native woods—and, when needed, *between* the habitat patches flanking each side of a busy freeway.

GREEN BRIDGES IN SOUTHEAST ASIA

When in 1986 the Bukit Timah Expressway (BKE) was completed in Singapore, the six-lane highway had cost several billion dollars to construct and it plowed through a wide swath of pristine rainforest. But there was another cost, too.

The critically endangered Sunda pangolin faced a lethal threat from the thousands of cars, trucks, and motorcycles powering down the expressway, leaving several pangolins and countless other forest creatures dead on the road each year. With the Bukit Timah Nature Reserve on one side and the Central Catchment Nature Reserve on the other, the BKE severed many wildlife populations: long-tailed macaques (not the lion-tails of India), emerald doves, and Asian palm civets, whose sinuous tail says "cat" and whose sharp masked face announces "racoon." Adjacent rock quarries and condos also pressed hard on these diminished, divided habitat patches.

Nature-loving Singaporeans—including scientists, National Parks Board officials, and local students—knew they had to do something to help stop the roadkills, minimize the barrier effect, and prevent the local extinction of native species, like the cream-coloured giant squirrel and Smith's green-eyed gecko, both of which vanished from the reserves in the wake of the BKE. A strong coalition of wildlife advocates embarked on the kind of careful planning we saw in Chapter 3. They used camera traps, on-the-ground wildlife surveys, and even information-gathering trips to green bridges in Switzerland and the Netherlands. In 2013, the forest was finally reconnected.

The Eco-Link@BKE is the first mega wildlife bridge we've visited thus far, and one of the largest in the world at 203 feet (62 meters) long, with an elegant hourglass shape. The wide entrances to the overpass fan out into the neighboring vegetation like open arms, welcoming animals to continue on their journeys—or stop for a snack or a rest.

Like the much smaller golden lion tamarin overpass in Brazil, the Eco-Link is a truly living bridge, with dense shrubs to shelter shrew-faced squirrels and insect-rich undergrowth for the pint-size glossy horseshoe bat. Thick vegetation lines the edges to block and absorb light, heat, and traffic noise. Deep soil invites scaly, sharp-clawed Sunda pangolins to dig for the ants and termites they crave.

And just as the Brazilian tamarin bridge fosters trees to attract vulnerable primates, the Eco-Link is also a forested bridge. Native palms and Seashore Mangosteen trees shoot upward to entice long-tailed macaques, as well as other primates such as Malayan colugos, who glide through the canopy like their fellow rainforest tree dwellers, the red-cheeked flying squirrel.

The Eco-Link@BKE continues to shield the rare Sunda pangolin and other threatened wildlife from the roaring expressway, as well as to reconnect two pivotal nature reserves. It has since inspired Singapore's second major wildlife crossing project. The Mandai Wildlife Bridge, completed in 2019, is even longer than its predecessor, stretching across busy Mandai Lake Road to re-link fragments of the Central Catchment Nature Reserve, also sliced apart by the Bukit Timah Expressway.

Richly vegetated and replete with the kinds of faunal furniture we saw in Australia's Slaty Creek Wildlife Underpass, the Mandai overcrossing is hosting many of the species that traverse the Eco-Link, with at least one very encouraging addition. Red-listed by the International Union for Conservation of Nature (IUCN) as "vulnerable," shaggy, nocturnal sambar deer visit the structure nearly every night, and camera trap footage has even captured two young males locking antlers in a mid-bridge scuffle.

Camera traps have also, though, ensnared human interlopers on the Mandai Wildlife Bridge. Part of every wildlife crossing proposal is the question of *our* access. Some structures, including one we'll tour shortly, may harmoniously integrate some human use. But most scientists agree that wildlife culverts, ecoducts, and underpasses should be exactly that: *just* for wildlife. Especially for shy creatures like pangolins and palm civets, our presence and lingering scent can discourage them from entering, let alone crossing the bridges to safety that we've worked so hard to plan, design, fund, and build.

The teams behind Singapore's celebrated Mandai Wildlife Bridge and Eco-Link@BKE decided that, except for enjoying a few naturalist-guided walks a year, the public can best appreciate from afar the wildlife that they're helping save. Stiff fines greet those trespassers who disagree. Wherever we are, we can join the conservationists—professional scientists and caring citizens—of Singapore in respecting wild creatures' need for space, in which to travel, grab a meal, or simply exist.

SHARING AN ECODUCT IN THE NETHERLANDS

Wildlife crossings are creating larger coexistence zones for the people and primates of India's Western Ghats, the elephants and farmers of Kenya's Mount Kenya, and the urban wildlife and human city dwellers of Southern California. Yet residents of Hilversum in the Netherlands have created such a zone actually *on* their wildlife overpass, which they call an ecoduct.

Completed in 2006, the Natuurbrug Zanderij Crailoo is currently the largest wildlife crossing in the world. At 2,625 feet (800 meters) long and 164 feet (50 meters) wide, this expansive structure spans a river, a bustling highway, a major rail line, a business complex, and even a sports center. Like Singapore's Eco-Link@BKE, the Zanderij Crailoo bridge reconnects severed nature reserves that are themselves islands within a heavily developed (*disturbed*) landscape.

Local wildlife like red foxes, sand lizards, and European

hares, inhabiting isolated patches of forests and heaths, needed room to roam. But in this heavily populated province of North Holland, so did human residents, who love biking, hiking, birdwatching, and horseback riding. In 1995, when concern about roadkill and habitat fragmentation spurred talk of a wildlife bridge in Hilversum, public support for a multimillion dollar ecoduct wasn't exactly robust—until transportation experts and government officials proposed a "co-use" model. To the Netherlands' great credit, hundreds of wildlife tunnels and overpasses, many just for animals, now crisscross the land, becoming as iconic as tulips and windmills.

While road ecologists and wildlife experts largely discourage multiuse structures, the designers, engineers, and wildlife biologists developing the Natuurbrug Zanderij Crailoo found ingenious ways to please nature lovers wanting to explore both reserves flanking the road *and* to give creatures on the move links to needed habitat. We all, it seems, crave connectivity!

First of all, the largest section of the bridge belongs to the roe deer, field voles, and foraging birds and bats. Hikers, bikers, and equestrians mustn't venture beyond relatively narrow trails that are securely separated from the critters' territory with buffer zones: earth berms, dense vegetation, fencing, and other "screening" materials. And the wildlife's real estate includes all the wonderful features of the best green bridges: rocks and shrubbery to shelter grass snakes and rabbits, flowering plants for the gorgeous Alcon blue butterfly to pollinate, small ponds to entice moor frogs, pine and birch trees for red squirrels to climb, and huckleberry bushes for browsing roe deer.

Moreover, the bridge and the nature reserves themselves are closed to the (human) public at sundown, when many creatures are just beginning to venture out for dinner or some social time. Over one hundred eighty thousand people a year enjoy the fresh air and greenery of the ecoduct and, with a few exceptions, stay in their own lane, keeping the rest of the perfectly named Nature Bridge free and clear for the wildlife who most need it.

Two native species, badgers and pine martens, faced a particularly bleak future as habitat disappeared and splintered in and around Hilversum. In fact, ecologist Edgar van der Grift informs me that these remarkable little mammals had been absent from the reserves for many decades. Now, thanks to the overpass, both creatures have recolonized the once-divided forest. It's wonderful to see a melancholy story of local extinction blossom into a heartening tale of return and recovery—and to imagine sleek pine martens peering into the evening mist from atop the bridge's oak trees while a striped, low-slung badger burrows into the rich soil below.

Long-term monitoring of the thoughtfully designed Natuurbrug Zanderij Crailoo has shown that wild creatures can sometimes cross the road together with us, as long as our parallel paths never crowd one another.

GRIZZLIES, WOLVES, AND BIGHORN SHEEP FINDING CONNECTIONS IN CANADA

Touching down in the boreal forest of Western Canada, we'll now venture into the rugged terrain of the Rocky Mountains.

Yet even here, in the wilderness of Banff National Park, home to some of the world's most iconic megafauna, the human footprint—or roadprint—is never far away.

One stretch of the Trans-Canada Highway (TCH) that tears through the park earned the grisly nickname "The Meat Maker" because of its deadly record of wildlife-vehicle collisions, including a hundred a year involving elk. While the sleepy road in California's Prairie Creek Redwoods State Park posed little danger to those nonchalant Roosevelt elk ambling across the pavement, the busy TCH was no match for Banff's antlered monarchs—or for the bears, moose, wolves, and lynx that roam its craggy peaks, evergreen forests, and lush meadows.

Though road expansion inevitably chews up more land, a highway-widening project in the 1980s also brought relief for both TCH motorists and the park's wild creatures when Parks Canada launched what became the world's largest and most varied wildlife crossing system. Unlike in Hilversum, Holland, wildlife-only bridges are the name of the game here in Banff.

As wildlife biologists tracked animal movements and pinpointed roadkill hot spots, they also explored the larger corridors that, for example, wide-ranging grizzly bears travel as they follow patches of ripening berries and through which elk migrate as they move seasonally between alpine meadows and valley bottoms. These corridors would need to flow naturally into the culverts, tunnels, and overpasses that would carry animals across a four-lane highway that sees over twenty-six thousand cars, trucks, and RVs *per day* during the

summer tourist season. Carnivores like coyotes and cougars, herbivores (plant-eaters) such as moose and bighorn sheep, small mammals, including porcupines and voles, and endangered fliers like barn swallows and little brown bats all needed bridges to safety and to more expansive ranges.

After engineers began tunneling under roads and raising bridges aloft, scientists could watch camera-trap wildlife selfies that told the story of species preferences. Deer and elk, they learned, definitely do *not* like dark tunnels, though black bears appreciate their shadowy recesses. And grizzlies agree with their hoofed neighbors that high, wide, and bright is the way to go. Thus the creatures themselves are the ultimate crossing experts, helping the road ecologists, biologists, and transportation officials decide not just *where* to build bridges, but also what *kinds* to construct.

Though some animals, including reclusive carnivores like wolves, were initially reluctant to enter the structures, elk crossed them immediately, forging a path for the eleven species of large mammals that would find safe passage across the highway. Small creatures like garter snakes and boreal toads travel across as well. And mother black bears and grizzlies are teaching their young to use and to *trust* the once-strange structures in their forest home.

Now, with forty-four crossings, including six overpasses, and miles of sturdy exclusion fencing, Canada's oldest national park has reduced wildlife-vehicle collisions by more than 80 percent. Moreover, by reconnecting habitat patches, the bridges also allow the park's famed grizzlies, for example, to intermingle more freely and avoid the genetic disasters spawned by inbreeding. The crossing system has not, however, eliminated occasional "bear jams," when motorists stop to gawk at a grizzly or black bear near the roadside!

Banff National Park's overpasses, the only crossings visible to drivers, are especially beautiful. With two graceful arches crowned with shrubs and conifers, the bridges seem hewn from the rocky peaks that tower around them and artfully fashioned by nature itself. And though not the showpieces of travel brochures and nature documentaries, Banff's camouflaged culverts and other hidden underpasses also offer critical shelter and connectivity to a whole host of creatures.

One unusual and unsung bridge, within the park but not part of its highway crossings system, reminds us that other infrastructure, not just roads, can block wildlife movement. Two Jack Canal, which carries water from a lake to a local hydropower station, posed an impenetrable barrier to bighorn sheep and deer, as well as to carnivores like foxes and cougars. Teaming up to help stranded wildlife, Parks Canada and the local utility company came up with an innovative, inexpensive, and environmentally sustainable solution. They recycled/repurposed three flat-deck railway cars that could bridge the canal. Covered with native foliage, these cars now carry a new kind of precious cargo, including elk, wolves, bears of each species, and a number of smaller travelers such as snowshoe hares, weasels, and red squirrels. Canada geese, who could easily fly across the water, enjoy just hanging out on the bridge and nibbling grass.

If the BDFFP stands as Earth's largest laboratory of habitat fragmentation, Banff National Park is conducting the world's grandest experiment in ecological connectivity. Every year, hundreds of scientists, conservationists, and landscape architects from around the globe make pilgrimages to this Canadian boreal forest, where a marvelous crossings system is helping save an irreplaceable ecosystem. Park officials have hosted biologists and transportation experts from China, Mongolia, and Argentina, as well as visitors from the Confederated Salish and Kootenai Tribes of the Flathead Reservation, who were eager to learn how to create grizzly crossings on their reservation.

In Banff National Park, some of North America's most charismatic creatures—grizzlies, wolves, and bighorn sheep—along with the forest's less celebrated inhabitants, are making their way unimpeded across a once-deadly highway and a man-made canal, lighting the way for other wild travelers who urgently need open pathways, not harmful roadblocks.

CHAPTER 6
BRIDGING TRAFFIC IN SOUTHERN CALIFORNIA: A CELEBRITY MOUNTAIN LION AND HIS HUMAN ENTOURAGE

Biggest. Most expensive. Straddling one of the United States' busiest freeways. Bordering the nation's second most populous city—and inspired by one famous big cat.

Superlatives surround the Wallis Annenberg Wildlife Crossing, the culmination of decades of work and open for business in 2025. Innovative and often beautiful wildlife crossing structures, curving over and dipping under dangerous roadways, have become a global phenomenon, and with their dramatic video footage, an Internet sensation. But the Wallis Annenberg Wildlife Crossing will be a crowning achievement in engineering, landscape architecture, and, of course, wildlife conservation. Even before a mountain lion, brush rabbit, or western toad sets foot on the bridge, folks around the globe are tuning in to the webcam that is live streaming the construction process itself!

We're back in Liberty Canyon, where the 101 Freeway severs two populations of the region's most charismatic species, as well as isolates and too often slaughters other native creatures who brave the endless stream of traffic. Car strikes and inbreeding, as well as ingestion of rodenticide, threaten to push Southern California's remaining mountain lions into oblivion. But a brilliantly designed wildlife superhighway brings real hope to these apex carnivores and to all the less celebrated members of this extraordinary ecosystem.

Thirty-six miles (58 kilometers) north of Los Angeles's city center, the overpass will stretch 210 feet (64 meters) with a width of 175 ft (53 meters). Though these dimensions may not sound as impressive as those of the Natuurbrug Zanderij Crailoo, the colossal Wallis Annenberg bridge will, in fact, be the world's largest crossing structure dedicated solely to wildlife (recall that people also use the Hilversum overcrossing).

Thirty carefully chosen native plant species will bedeck the bridge and flow into the adjacent slopes and ridges. Painstakingly planting five thousand individual plants on the crossing itself, landscapers will then clothe the structure's adjoining 12 acres (about 9 hectares) with *sixty thousand* shrubs, grasses, perennials, and forbs (herbaceous flowering plants, or wildflowers). Yet fun facts and stats, including a $92-million-dollar price tag, don't capture the Hollywood-worthy stories, and cast of characters, behind this epic project.

We'll start with the big cat. Recall P-22's hazardous trek from his home range in the Santa Monica Mountains to the urban enclave of Griffith Park. But why did he leave home in the first place? At about two years of age, P-22 made the kind of dispersal journey, to find his own territory and mate, common to all young male, and some female, cougars. Wide-ranging and fiercely territorial, these big cats simply cannot hang out on their original home turf once they reach adulthood.

Like the star of a superhero movie, P-22 beat incredible odds by surviving a maze of dangerous obstacles, including the notorious LA traffic racing along the two mammoth freeways he traversed. The bridge at Liberty Canyon will help ensure that his fellow mountain lions, and other native wildlife, won't have to be so heroic—or just plain lucky—when they embark on their own travels.

As P-22's captivating story, and gorgeous camera-trap photos, made headline news, first in Los Angeles and then worldwide, longtime efforts to build a wildlife bridge in Liberty Canyon finally started to pay off, with the public fired up and donations pouring in. So while the seeds for this green bridge had been planted decades earlier, P-22's saga is bringing the project to fruition.

His story offers both triumph and a bit of melancholy. P-22 found no partner in his new habitat, which at 9 square miles (23 square kilometers) is the smallest known home range for a male mountain lion, who usually need about 150 square miles (389 square kilometers) to roam. Marvelously handsome, with mesmerizing kohl-rimmed eyes peering from his tawny face and sporting a GPS collar, P-22 remained a bachelor. It wasn't safe to relocate him or import a mate to Griffith Park. Someone would have ended up badly hurt, or worse.

We know so much about P-22 thanks to two experts on urban carnivores, both with the National Parks Service: Dr. Seth Riley and Jeff Sikich, who tracked P-22 since his arrival in Griffith Park. In fact, Sikich actually, and safely, tranquilized and trapped the big guy to fit him with his first radio collar, and later replaced his collars six times when the batteries conked out! He and Dr. Riley also doctored P-22 when the cat came down with a nasty case of mange after ingesting rodenticide.

Sikich, who praises P-22 as "a great ambassador for urban wildlife and the need for connectivity," calls it "such a privilege" and genuinely "amazing" to have handled the massive feline. He describes the experience as "a task that I take very seriously. I am responsible for that captured animal's safety, so I work very quickly and efficiently." Sikich also reminds us that in a small park with millions of visitors, P-22 has rarely been seen: "His secretive and elusive nature lives up to the nickname 'ghost cat!'"

We'll now meet the remarkable conservation champion who has done the most to broadcast P-22's story and to bring the Liberty Canyon crossing project from a wildly ambitious dream to its imminent reality. Not long after fellow scientist Michael Ordeñana first spotted the cougar on candid camera, Sikich invited California's Regional Executive Director of the National Wildlife Federation Beth Pratt to meet him on P-22's Griffith Park turf. He and Dr. Riley also showed her the site, staked out decades before, for a possible wildlife bridge spanning the Liberty Canyon section of the 101 Freeway. For Pratt, these two visits were revelatory. That bridge absolutely must be built, she thought, and P-22 could help the public understand why.

Thanks both to Pratt's incredible work as his public relations manager and stunning images taken by famed *National Geographic* photographer Steve Winter, P-22 became the glamorous poster cat for #SaveLACougars, which would raise millions of dollars to fund what some locals call "the mountain lion bridge." Songs, murals, T-shirts, a museum exhibit, and an annual P-22 Day Festival celebrate his life and his amazing journey and remind us that a bridge to the wilderness near his original home turf would have made that treacherous trek unnecessary.

Pratt, who leads the #SaveLACougars campaign, has been fighting for wild creatures, and open land, since she was seven, when she offered a local landowner $5 for a parcel of woods destined for the chainsaw. (Sadly, he turned her down.) Moved by P-22's courage and his tragic separation from his kind, Pratt has tirelessly shepherded the overpass project, fundraising, educating, and advocating.

Sporting an impressive P-22 tattoo on her left arm, stashing cougar plushies in her car for potential #SaveLACougars supporters, and tagging herself "P-22's BFF" on a recent Zoom call, Pratt finds herself most involved with the plight of mountain lions, threatened with local extinction. Yet wildlife bridges less grand than the Liberty Canyon overpass and critters less conventionally charismatic than cougars have also captured her heart.

These days, she finds herself especially inspired by crossings for the smaller creatures "just as impacted by the roads," like the amphibians who make good use of the "toad road" undercrossing near her home in Yosemite (recall Amherst's salamander tunnels!). And when she anticipates the completed Wallis Annenberg Wildlife Crossing, she likes to envision butterflies fluttering across, keeping good company with

P-22's cousins and other creatures on the move: "I love that this crossing will become a safe haven for butterflies making their annual journey near and far."

While cougars are clearly the bridge's target species, Tataviam and Chumash elder and storyteller Alan Salazar also likes to imagine coyotes making their way across, rescued by caring people, just as Coyote rescues Hawk in a traditional Chumash tale. Salazar has worked closely with Pratt for many years, educating both children and adults about local wildlife and the Southern and Central California mountains, foothills, and valleys that are his people's ancestral homeland. The Tataviam and Chumash "have always respected all of the animals, big and small," he tells me. They are our teachers, he continues, "and we are clan people. So, we have the mountain lion clan, eagle clan, and spider clan, to name a few. It has saddened our people when we see all of our relatives being killed by cars and trucks. So building a bridge is very important to us."

At a number of #SaveLACougars events, Salazar has told the moving story of the Rainbow Bridge, which the Earth Goddess Hutash made to help the Chumash people cross the sea to the mainland from their original island home. Like the Rainbow Bridge, he explains, the overpass at Liberty Canyon "will provide a safe way to cross a dangerous passage. For the Chumash people living on Limuw—Santa Cruz Island—the Rainbow Bridge allowed us to cross the ocean safely. This bridge will help our animal relatives cross the dangerous 101 highway.

Sharing Salazar's ideal of cultural as well as ecological connectivity, is landscape architect Robert Rock. His Chicago-based company, Living Habitats, is designing the bridge as well as overseeing the complex processes of selecting, propagating, and planting the native foliage that will bring the structure to life—and bring wildlife to the structure. Rock hopes both to keep mountain lions from "wandering into extinction" and to reconnect, restore, and revitalize the whole ecosystem surrounding the structure. "We are designing for the mountain lions," he tells me, but also "for the California king snake, the harvester ants, the coyote bush, the chaparral—supporting this complex series of species at all levels."

Rock is mindful of the bridge's symbolic power: "It serves our own need to restore connections that we have severed or have lost or did not understand when we disrupted them." Whether we live in a huge metropolis like Los Angeles or a more rural locale, wildlife crossings remind us to find our own bridges (back) to the natural world—the remote wilderness, as well as our backyard or neighborhood park.

Like the crossing team we observed in Chapter 3, Rock and his colleagues—botanists, soil specialists, structural engineers, sound and light experts, entomologists, to name just a few—are approaching their work from the animals' own point of view. As he designs key features of the Wallis Annenberg Wildlife Crossing, Rock imagines, for example, how the ground surface would feel to a slowly slithering gopher snake compared to a swiftly striding bobcat.

Different styles and speeds of movement and a variety of forage, moisture, and shelter needs: the whole green bridge team needs to keep these and other crucial factors in mind as they prepare the ground for their biodiverse clientele, the alligator lizards and mule deer, monarch butterflies and desert cottontails, golden eagles and, yes, mountain lions eagerly awaiting opening day.

As noted earlier, the Wallis Annenberg Wildlife Crossing won't include recreational trails. But embedded cameras will allow us to observe its wild visitors. The bridge will be similar to the space that ecologist Michelle Mariscal is cultivating and protecting in the Puente Hills Preserve, part of the same ecological hotspot that encompasses Liberty Canyon.

For indeed this overpass will be both a habitat *and* crossing structure, a truly living ecosystem. Part of a much larger nature preserve, it is the critical puzzle piece of an expansive wildlife corridor that will stretch far inland, from the Pacific coast to the rugged mountain sanctuary of Los Padres National Forest.

Beth Pratt sees the crossing, and especially the protected and restored land fanning out from both sides, as part of "an excellent climate-resiliency strategy" that will help animals (and plants) find refuge in a region dried and decimated by droughts and the kinds of fierce wildfires like the one that scorched the area in 2018.

When the Santa Monica Mountains and Simi Hills cougars meet at last, P-22's gift will be the pathway now opened for them and for the other native creatures stranded just a while longer on either side of a sea of traffic.

As we conclude this part of our ecological connectivity tour, let's remind ourselves what we're actually making when we build culverts, underpasses, and green bridges. We're creating a physical structure, yes, but we're also making up for what we've taken from wild creatures, making room for them to roam, reproduce, and thrive—and making sure that we, too, feel a part of the natural world that is our home.

It turns out that it's not just landscapes that need restoration and healing—and not just terrestrial species that must navigate patchy, degraded habitats. Bodies of water that thread through the world, and the wild creatures that rely on them, have also endured a long history of ecological devastation. Let's now see how *waterways* can become blocked and fragmented—and how we can help them flow freely, and naturally, once again.

CHAPTER 7
DOWN WITH DAMS

A chorus of voices echoes through the regional park near my Southern California home: the raspy screeches of a blue jay, the low drone of mosquitos, the quiet singing of a lively little stream that curves close to the trail I'm hiking.

As the path ends, so does the flow of the creek itself: the willows and sycamores flanking the creek disappear and a large sunlit pond comes into view. Just behind it a small dam looms, about twenty feet high, but large enough to block the water's movement. Gone are the delicate ripples and graceful meanders of the creek. An oily scum coats the surface of the water, as slimy algae floats in rancid patches and clings to the rocks that rim the shore.

The creek itself creates what's called a **riparian zone**. This is a lush natural homeland that hugs the banks of rivers and streams and radiates outward to embrace a whole wildlife community. In this park, that means raccoons and hummingbirds, kingfishers and aquatic insects, bobcats and even the occasional mountain lion. Also essential to and depending on riparian zones is another kind of wildlife that desperately needs the kind of connectivity we've been exploring, wildlife that swims rather than crawls, gallops, or hops.

I wonder whether the rock-and-concrete dam plugging the ravine creates a dead end for any fish traveling this small stream. A park ranger later tells me that local carp and blue-gill can, in fact, pass over the dam when the flow is high. How-ever, the stagnant pond itself, once used to irrigate nearby orchards, hints at a story told on a much larger scale by rivers and streams throughout the world. When blocked and frag-mented by dams, waterways—*lifeways* for fish—become indus-trial machines.

RAISING AND REMOVING THE BARRICADES

Dams have been part of human history for so long that they may seem like natural outgrowths of the landscape—or riverscape. Ancient Egyptians wedged the oldest large-scale dam into the Nile River over five thousand years ago. At just 46 feet (14 meters) tall and 371 feet (113 meters) long, the Sadd el-Kafara Dam barely hints at the enormous structures that now plug rivers across the globe: America's Hoover Dam, 726 feet (221 meters) tall, Switzerland's Grande Dixence Dam, 935 feet (285 meters) tall, and the current record holder, China's Jinping-I Dam, looming 1,001 feet (305 meters) above the Yalong River.

Around the globe, once wild and majestic rivers are har-nessed for hydroelectric power. This is created when confined water is pumped into spinning turbines, which then turn gen-erators that produce electricity. Many rivers are also siphoned into irrigation canals and transformed into giant water storage tanks. These large reservoirs, or artificial lakes, impound waterways the way that old-fashioned dog pounds (the words share the same root) once imprisoned pups.

Climate change, with its increasingly severe droughts and heat waves, only exacerbates the pressures we're putting on our rivers and, in turn, the wildlife that dwell within or near them. Advocates for the wild world and its wild creatures realize that the health, integrity, and connectivity of the natural world must include waterways as well as landscapes. If we are currently enjoying the Age of the Wildlife Crossing, as some journalists and conservationists claim, we may also be entering the Age of Dam Removal.

While we *make*—design and build—bridges to help terrestrial wildlife like Kenya's elephants and Singapore's pangolins roam safely, the billions of fish that travel the liquid highways crisscrossing the earth need something quite different. To open paths for aquatic species we must often *break*, actually demolish the dams that impede the movement not just of fish, but of the life-giving water itself.

At the forefront of the fight for dam removal, for free-flowing rivers, are Native communities, especially in the United States' Pacific Northwest, communities whose cultures and livelihood depend on healthy, connected rivers—and the fish who inhabit them. The Lower Elwha Klallam Tribe in Washington State and the Yurok Tribe and Karuk Tribe of California are bringing down the dams that clog their rivers and decimate the migratory salmon that have sustained their families for thousands of years. Their tireless work reminds us that to break means much more than to destroy. For the people, the fish, and the rivers themselves, dam removal means a *breakthrough*, an opening that, in turn, restores, renews, and re*makes* a whole ecosystem—and those who care for and depend on it.

Just as wildlife crossing projects need a broad coalition of scientists, policymakers, designers, and a dedicated, caring public to bring them to fruition, dam busting also demands cooperative efforts—and perhaps a theatrical flair. In 2011, a group of protesters graffitied a huge pair of scissors and a long perforated line down the front of the fish-blocking, aging Matilija Dam in Southern California. Now the conservation group California Trout (CalTrout) is partnering with other environmental organizations and state agencies to tear down this 168-feet-high (51 meters) wall of cement and release the long-confined Ventura River, which will once again flow freely to the Pacific Ocean.

The key beneficiaries of the restored river will be the endangered Southern California steelhead, a migratory fish that needs extensive, unbroken aquatic corridors just as desperately as Wyoming's pronghorn need their open plains and lion-tailed macaques their intact rainforests. Steelhead, like other salmonids (members of the salmon family), are **diadromous** fish, which means that they travel between fresh and salt water to grow, forage, and eventually spawn. Because steelhead need access both to the ocean and upper reaches of their home rivers, dams like the Matilija "short-circuit the life cycles" of these heroic migrators, as Dr. Sandra Jacobson, South Coast Regional Director of CalTrout puts it. Once the dam comes down, she continues, "the river will have freedom to roam," and so will the fish.

MIGRATORY FISH GET A BOOST

While Southern California's steelhead await the dam's opened floodgates, other fish around the world get a leg–or, rather, fin–up and over some of the barriers they encounter. Since at least the seventeenth century–when European anglers (fisherfolk) stacked branches alongside primitive dams–fish ladders, also called fishways, have helped fish swim, leap, and otherwise muscle their way up and over the impervious walls they literally bump up against. Although fish biologists stress that such contraptions can't substitute for the natural swimways of undammed rivers and streams, they do give migratory species such as steelhead and Chinook salmon a fighting chance.

As one study suggests, fish passage designers need to "think like a fish." Slope, water velocity, degree of turbulence, and access to the entrance all determine whether the target species will indeed be able to find and use such aquatic crossing structures.

The "pool and weir" style, featuring a series of ascending steps, is most common. But some fish actually ride elevators, or fish lifts, that lug them to the top of the dam and release them, like guests at a local water park, back into the river. Salmon cannons (!) get their piscine passengers past obstructions by sucking them into long tubes and shooting them over the dam, a gentle, nontraumatic ride, its inventor assures us. Finally, CalTrout is partnering with a group of hydraulic, civil, and structural engineers to create an intricate, vast fishway in Orange County, California. Its sequence of baffles, notches, and resting pools will guide the silvery steelhead and other fish not over a dam, but *under* a quarter-mile-long array of free-way and railroad bridges.

If these Southern California fish will be swimming beneath the highway once this incredible passageway opens for business, endangered Chinook and sockeye salmon have actually traveled *on* highways in California and Idaho, where climate change conspires with massive dams to obstruct their passage upstream to spawn.

Salmon, which spend much of their lives at sea, need very cold water; temperatures above 70 degrees Fahrenheit (21 Celsius) can, in fact, be deadly. Increasingly hot weather and seemingly endless drought have heated and depleted many of their waterways. Wildlife biologists often have to intercept salmon as they head into these treacherously warm waters. Captured at the foot of California's Eagle Canyon and Idaho's Lower Granite dams, Snake River sockeyes are packed into ice-water-filled tanks and onto trucks for a long road trip, 300 miles (483 kilometers), to upstream spawning grounds.

Clambering up fish ladders, crowding into elevators, whooshing through plastic cannons, hitching a ride on Fish and Wildlife Department pickup trucks: these somewhat absurd stopgap measures, which only rescue a small percentage of fish, rob noble, ancient migratory creatures of their self-sufficiency and their *wildness*. While some dams, are here to stay, devoted aquatic ecologists are chipping away at many of these barriers. They're unleashing imprisoned rivers, restoring countless miles of riparian habitat, and liberating millions of fish that will brave the rapids, drift the shallows, and find rest in the deep, shady pools of their own home waters.

SOUTH AFRICA'S KRUGER NATIONAL PARK: DEMOLISHING DAMS AND WELCOMING BACK EELS

Safari-goers in South Africa's Kruger National Park (KNP) are unlikely to be on the lookout for the various dams that dot the reserve's huge complex of waterways. Scanning the savannah for the "big five"—rhinos, elephants, buffalos, lions, and leopards—most visitors won't be preoccupied with the plight of indigenous fish species. When they do encounter, for instance, the Letaba River, it will be hippos and Nile crocodiles vying for their attention. But the Letaba is a critical aquatic ecosystem biodiversity hotspot, with over thirty fish species, many of them migratory, too many of them threatened. Flat-headed gobies, Mozambique tilapia, red-eyed mudfish, and bulldog fish roam the waters of the park, hidden to the casual visitor, but much on the minds of freshwater ecologist Robin Petersen and his KNP colleagues.

Petersen is part of an exciting restoration program that's undoing years of damage wrought by the government's ill-conceived "water-for-game" program, which installed numerous troughs, concrete reservoirs, and dams throughout the park between 1930 and 1990. Meant to help KNP's wildlife during drought, these artificial watering holes wreaked havoc on the surrounding vegetation, thus robbing animals of the food that should have sustained them year-round.

As Petersen tells me, instead of ranging through whole landscapes as they had in the past, snacking and sipping and moving on, jumbo-size herbivores such as elephants, buffalo, and giraffes began "camping out," trampling and gobbling up plants and intimidating rarer, more retiring species like roan and sable antelopes. Wildlife, as you know, are natural wanderers, and the dams, with their too-convenient water supplies, were turning the park's most iconic creatures into hulking bullies and couch potatoes.

And, just as such barriers do elsewhere, KNP's dams were chopping up rivers and blocking the ancient swimways of the park's aquatic inhabitants. Just a few years ago, KNP, South Africa's first and largest national park (about the size of Israel), also became the first in Africa to remove dams for ecological reasons. With the goal of restoring free-flowing rivers, officials have already demolished twenty-two of the park's fifty-three dams. And elephants and lions, zebras and jackals are once again seeking out naturally occurring water sources, spread throughout the park as part of their ancient travel routes. Roaming instead of lingering, KNP's animals are rediscovering their wildness, just as its rivers are.

While you won't find any tigers in Kruger National Park, you will find the African tiger fish, a fierce predator brandishing lethal-grade teeth. The only freshwater fish known to snatch birds right out of the air, tiger fish need unobstructed liquid highways as they move seasonally between colder and warmer reaches of their home rivers. Though the numerous man-made barriers reduced their numbers over the years, tiger fish are thankfully rebounding in the wake of ongoing dam removals.

One bird that this incredible fish won't be feasting on is the African fish eagle, who swoops down from her riverside perch, snagging fish with powerful barbed talons. Boasting an impressive wingspan, gorgeous white hood, and piercing cry, this majestic raptor is just one of many avian and terrestrial species that the park's freely running rivers will support—with more wholesome waters and more abundant prey.

Petersen tells me of an unusual partnership forged by KNP's dam-busting project. In 1988, thirteen years after the Kanniedood Dam impounded the Shingwedzi River, nineteen native fish species had disappeared downstream and another thirteen were absent upstream. Only 26 feet (8 meters) high, the Kanniedood was harming fish just as severely as any mega-dam. When in 2018, it was time for the Kanniedood to go, the park enlisted the military. The South African National Defense Force needed demolition training, the fish needed their river back, and the huge explosion ignited by the army (loudly) announced a new era for the Shingwedzi.

As he discusses the aquatic creatures that swim through KNP, Petersen exudes an especially warm affection for African longfin and mottled eels. And, yes, eels are indeed fish, though they look a lot like shiny snakes, with narrow snouts, long undulating bodies, and nearly invisible fins. Diadromous African eels begin life in the Indian Ocean, then swim far distances through inland rivers, finally taking the reverse journey seaward to spawn. (Steelhead, sockeyes, and other salmonids follow an opposite trajectory.) Like other migratory fish, eels are important indicator species, signaling the health and connectivity—or lack thereof—of both the oceans and the rivers they inhabit.

The presence or absence of dams, Petersen explains, has very much determined the fate of the eels within the park. Eels have continued to thrive within the largely undammed

Crocodile River, which indeed swarms with these fear-some beasts. But until the Kanniedood Dam came down, the Shingwedzi River was missing both mottled and longfin eels. In a big win for river restoration, as Petersen puts it, eels are finally returning to the river as part of their epic journey from the faraway Indian Ocean.

Home to the critically endangered black and white rhinos, Kruger National Park is also regaining its role as a safe haven for threatened African eels as, one by one, its dams disappear, sometimes in the smoke of well-deployed sticks of dynamite. The park's visitors, eager to glimpse a graceful leopard or tow-ering giraffe, probably know little about the African eels and other subtropical fish that travel the park's watery corridors. A conversation with aquatic ecologist and eel BFF Robin Petersen would definitely convince them that the story of these extraor-dinary creatures, and of the now-crumbling dams that once impeded them, is well worth telling.

SWEETFISH AND SALMON RUN THE RIVERS OF JAPAN

While Kruger National Park has staged Africa's very first dam demolition, the Kuma-gawa (or Kuma) River now winds its way more freely through Kyushu, Japan's southernmost main island, thanks to Asia's first major dam removal. Erected in 1954 near Sakamoto Village, the 82-foot-high (25 meters) Arase Dam provided hydroelectric power to the region. But it also destroyed the river's ecosystem as well as the livelihood of the fisherfolk who depended on the famed ayu, or sweetfish—and over forty-three other species that once flourished there.

An important waterbird habitat, the Kuma River began to see its ducks, plovers, and curlews vanish from its shores, underscoring that dams devastate whole riparian zones. A complicated and expensive process of capturing and trucking ayu fry (juvenile fish) upstream may remind us of their Idaho and California counterparts, shipped long distances in a desperate end run around impassible dams.

The tale of the Arase Dam and its ultimate demise brings the role of the **estuary**, the coastal wetlands at the mouth of a river, into sharp focus. Like every dam around the world, the Arase trapped tons of sediment and nutrients that would otherwise flow to the sea, replenishing the river's downstream reaches and, ultimately, the beach at Yatsushiro Bay, 12.5 miles (20 kilometers) from the dam. Prawns, crabs, and clams disappeared from the impoverished tidal zone, and even the vibrantly green seaweed began to die.

After years-long grassroots protests by conservationists, fisherfolk, and residents of Sakamoto Village, the process of dismantling the Arase Dam began in 2012. Villagers soon gathered in front of the detested structure for a celebratory photo op, holding up a colorful sign announcing in Japanese, GOODBYE! ARASE DAM. By 2018, when the last piles of rubble were hauled away, the Kuma River—and the estuary—was again pulsing with life. The sweetfish are rebounding, the shorebirds are flocking, and the ghost shrimp are no longer actual ghosts, but plump crustaceans burrowing in the bay's thick, nutrient-rich mud. Even long-absent eels are returning to the reconnected river. Robin Petersen would be delighted.

About 1,056 miles (1,700 kilometers) from Kyushu's Kuma

River, on Japan's northernmost island, Hokkaido, hundreds of small but harmful dams constrict, obstruct, and tame many of the rivers winding through the remote wilderness of Shiretoko Peninsula.

Deemed "the end of the Earth"—or *sir etok*—by the island's Indigenous Ainu people, this lushly wooded region juts into the Sea of Okhotsk. Here orcas, spotted seals, and beaked whales cruise icy waters. The world's largest owl, the endangered Blakiston's fish owl, patrols the peninsula's countless rivers and streams, an almost mythic "symbol of true wilderness," as its greatest expert and champion, Dr. Jonathan Slaght, puts it.

This is salmon country, and the Rusha River—home to chum, masu, and pink salmon—is now slowly regaining its freedom to roam.

As workers steadily chip away at a series of small dams that has clogged the river since the 1970s, scientists like research ecologist and salmon expert Dr. Peter Rand of Alaska's Prince William Sound Science Center have been carefully monitoring the Rusha. They note gradual increases in, for example, the pink salmon that provide tasty meals for the region's brown bears. Although Dr. Rand and colleagues like fisheries scientist Dr. Masahide Kaeriyama of Hokkaido University would like to see even more progress, dams that have been lowered or notched, or that now have fishways, are finally allowing more migrating fish to move upstream to spawn.

Dr. Rand sees dam removal and the connectivity it's restoring as a real boon for two of his own cherished Rusha River inhabitants: the raindrop patterned white-spotted char (known locally as ame masu, or rain salmon) and the "showy,

colorful" Dolly Varden char, both salmonids, like sockeyes and steelheads.

For Dr. Kaeriyama, understanding and protecting the fish of the Rusha River means treasuring the peninsula's entire eco-system. For him, the glossy green leaves and delicate white flowers of the endemic, and endangered, Shiretoko violet ("Shiretoko-sumire" in Japanese) and the regal plumage and hunting prowess of the massive Steller's sea eagle are emblem-atic of the region's irreplaceable natural heritage. The dams that, in Dr. Kaeriyama's words, "impede the ecological role of rivers as sea and land corridors" must, therefore, continue to fall. Then, and only then, can the naturally, wildly running rivers that once braided through Shiretoko Peninsula redis-cover their ancient paths.

If rain salmon and other migratory fish are cornerstones of these two scientists' work, they are also, in fact, **keystone species** in the region, creatures on whom all other life depends. Thus it's especially crucial that the Rusha River dams be demolished. Spending much of their lives at sea, the Dolly Varden, ame masu, and pink salmon import marine nutri-ents into rivers and streams and even the forest itself when they return to spawn. Incredible athletes with an extraordi-nary homing instinct, these salmonids must brave treacher-ous currents, navigate deep-water wood debris, and leap up waterfalls as high as ten feet. They must also dodge predators as they muscle their way to the very same freshwater spawn-ing grounds where they hatched. (You can understand why a gauntlet of dams is the last thing these intrepid travelers need!)

Yet death, perhaps in the jaws of the hulking Ussuri brown

bear, is inevitable for the returning fish. They are "programmed" to expire at journey's end; they stop feeding as they move from ocean to estuary to river, and they may even begin decaying well before their hearts stop beating. Passing through the guts of a bear or sea eagle or rotting in the shallows of a stream, the salmon of Shiretoko National Park help build the riparian forest. This forest, in turn, provides shade and insects for the young salmon that will hatch and grow in the coming months.

All along the banks of the Rusha, streamside willows are nourished by what ecologists call the marine-derived nutrients (MDNs) carried many miles within the salmons' ultimately lifeless, but still life-giving, bodies. The park's indigenous sika deer browsing these trees are in a very real sense being fed by the salmon! When brown bears snag a juicy fish, they often drag it far from shore, eventually leaving half-eaten carcasses to feed scavengers and insects and vegetation within the forest's interior. And, of course, salmon also fertilize the forest when bears and other fish-devouring wildlife leave their droppings streamside or in the wider riparian zone.

Consuming plankton and smaller fish in the sea, then swimming back to fresh waters to gift ocean nutrients to rivers, forests, and wild creatures, salmon do not only *need* unimpeded aquatic corridors. As living links between sea, river, and land, they actually, and poignantly, *embody* connectivity itself. In the mystical twilight of Shiretoko, a Blakiston's fish owl peers down at the Rusha River, watching with piercing yellow eyes as the dams fade into history and the rain salmon surge upstream, ready to spawn, ready to give their lives to the forest at the end of the Earth.

REDWOOD WATERWAYS AND NATIVE LIFEWAYS: CALIFORNIA'S KLAMATH RIVER

Drifting down Alaska's Kenai River in early autumn, I'm bathed in color. But neither the sapphire sky, golden birches, steel gray-blue water, silty with glacial flour, nor even the florescent pink life jacket of my companion can compete with the sea of red that engulfs our little boat. Hundreds of scarlet sockeye salmon are making their way upstream from the ocean. This is the culmination of what's called their "fall run," a perfect confluence of space (the river), time (the season), and life (the fish themselves).

Some press forward with great energy, while others barely withstand the gentle current. These last migrators, many with tattered fins and the hooked snouts and exposed teeth of the spawning male, are "zombie fish." They're hardly even alive, yet they're still following a genetically embedded GPS and the smell of their birthplace, where they'll breed a new generation of sockeye.

All along the shore are carcasses of the zombies that didn't complete their journey, and that will invite the Kenai's otters, lynx, and wolves to feast to their heart's content. The enormous grizzlies that roam the forest will, like the Ussuri brown bears of Shiretoko, expertly capture the vigorous swimmers, or, in a lazier mood, snack on the sockeye smorgasbord covering the river's banks.

The Kenai River runs free, untrammeled by any dams, which helps account for the multitude of sockeye, Dolly Varden, and coho salmon that find safe passage in its main channel and tributaries. Even the sluggish zombie fish and decomposing bodies washed ashore are signs of life here in this Alaskan paradise.

In September 2002, a much grimmer spectacle of dead fish greeted the Yurok Tribe of Northern California's coast redwoods region, 3,000 miles (4,800 kilometers) south of the Kenai. These fish met their gruesome end in a waterway cluttered and clogged by immense dams. The once majestic Klamath River became lethally warm, shallow, and disease-ridden when the U.S. government diverted water to upriver farms and ranches. More than thirty-four thousand Chinook or "king" salmon perished in the largest fish kill in United States history.

The Kenai sockeyes that my friend and I saw littering the shore died naturally, having reached–or nearly reached–their spawning pools. But the horrific carnage of the Klamath was very much an unnatural disaster, striking the fish at the start of their run, thus obliterating not "just" these several thousand, but the next generation as well.

The 2002 fish kill was the climax in a string of tragic injustices befalling the region's Yurok, Karuk, Klamath, and Hoopa Valley Nations since white loggers, gold miners, and home-steaders seized and desecrated the river and the old-growth redwood forest that is now merely a shadow of its ancient majesty. Since time immemorial, the Klamath River and its salmon have fed, literally and spiritually, the Indigenous people who have, in turn, loved and protected them. Yurok, in fact, means "downriver people," and salmon have provided them food, spiritual sustenance, and cultural identity for thousands of years.

An 1855 treaty with the U.S. government promised the Yurok Nation perpetual fishing rights, but the construction of several

dams in essence broke that agreement by impounding, siphon-
ing, and polluting the waters critical to the salmon and to the
people. Stagnant, tepid reservoirs and climate-change-fueled
heat and drought have only worsened the plight of the steelhead and salmon, who perish in ever-warming waters.

Although dams had been blocking fish passage, diverting
water, and fostering toxic algae blooms since 1918, it was the
catastrophic fish kill that really ignited the movement Un-Dam
the Klamath. Tribal members protested alongside allies from
the environmental and scientific communities, brandishing
signs that read DAMS KILL MORE THAN FISH and FIRST THE BUFFALO—NOW
THE SALMON.

Unlike the dam removals that we've looked at in South
Africa and Japan, the fight to dismantle the dams of the
Klamath has human rights, as well as wildlife protection, at
its center. Those fighting to free the Klamath are also battling
what's called **environmental injustice**, wherein the mistreat-
ment of the natural world and of vulnerable communities, usually people of color, goes hand in hand. Justice for the Klamath
River must then mean justice—and real healing—for the Native
communities who inhabit its shores. As new swimways open for
the river's salmon, ancestral lifeways of the Klamath region's
tribes will then find renewal and restoration.

After over twenty years of protests and court battles, the
world's most ambitious dam dismantling project has finally
begun. The demise of four hulking barriers, including the aptly
named Iron Gate, will open over 400 miles (644 kilometers) of
new habitat for salmon, including the majestic Chinook, that will
regain its status as the reigning king of the Klamath. In 2021,

U.S. Secretary of the Interior Deb Haaland, the nation's first Native American (Laguna Pueblo) to hold this position, wrote in a letter supporting dam demolition, "The Indian Tribes of the [Klamath] Basin have been sustained by the River's bounty since time immemorial. . . . Today, we have an incredible opportunity to restore this magnificent River" and "rewrite a painful chapter in our history."

Protecting the river and its salmon and guiding other young people in the Yurok Nation is Sammy Gensaw III, who at seventeen founded with his fourteen-year-old brother, Jon Luke, a group that teaches children and teens tribal history and sustainable fishing practices. Thus, the Gensaw brothers are helping their peers gain the kind of intimate knowledge of the river that has enriched their own lives. The Ancestral Guard grew out of the elder brother's work with Un-Dam the Klamath, where he served as a student-coalition community organizer.

Though the waters and forests of the Yurok Tribe will always be his home, Sammy Gensaw has traveled to a power company shareholders meeting in Nebraska to protest the dams. He even met with Indigenous leaders in Brazil and Malaysia who were facing their own dam-created crises. Cherishing the history and ancestry of his people, Gensaw is forging ahead, helping other young tribal members prepare for the river's liberation, the return of the salmon, the renewal of life and hope on the reservation. "The industrial revolution is over," he declares. "It's the restorative revolution now."

An astonishing promise of renewal recently arrived in Yurok territory in the unlikely form of a shaggy, prehistoric-looking bird. Nearly extinct in the 1980s, the California condor is roosting in the coastal redwoods and soaring above the Klamath for the first time in over 130 years. Nurtured in captivity as part of a program pairing the Yurok Tribe and Redwood National Park, four young condors were recently released into the wild.

Displaying a wingspan of up to 10 feet (3 meters), the Prey-go-neesh (the condor's Yurok name) wields a powerful beak that can rip through the toughest hides of the carcasses it scavenges, leaving remnants for smaller creatures who otherwise wouldn't be able to feed on the bodies of large animals like seals or elk. Tiana Williams-Claussen, Director of the Yurok Tribe Wildlife Society, sees the condor as "central in helping clean up the world and keep it in balance." Moreover, she explains, "We believe that he carries our prayers to the heavens when we're asking for the world to be in balance because they actually fly higher than any other bird in the system." These four young birds, with more to be released yearly, are reopening the skies above the Klamath, heralding the day when the waters will once again flow freely, replete with salmon, blessing the people.

About 600 miles (970 kilometers) north of Yurok lands, another tribe has already seen a once-entrapped-and-depleted river unleashed, welcoming back the salmon and restoring the land. For the Lower Elwha Klallam Tribe of Washington State's Olympic Peninsula, two huge hydroelectric dams erected more than a century ago spelled disaster for the salmon, the community, and the whole ecosystem. With the kinds of strong alliances and incredible tenacity that the Yurok Tribe is bringing to the battle, the Indigenous people of the

Elwha River brought down their own behemoths between 2011 and 2014, a long, gradual process that involved wrecking balls and explosives, revegetation and "rewilding" of drained reservoirs, and reintroduction of fish upstream.

The days of the one-hundred-pound "June hogs," enormous Chinook salmon making their summer Elwha run, may be over, but the river has come alive, flowing unimpeded from its mountain source to its mouth in the Strait of Juan de Fuca. The regenerated Elwha River is the promise of what a liberated Klamath River can be.

Kenai, Klamath, Elwha. These names remind us that the rivers, with their iconic Pacific salmon, are ancestral waters, known and loved and stewarded for thousands of years by the tribes that continue to inhabit their shores. ELWHA BE FREE boldly commanded the words inscribed on the face of the now-departed Elwha Dam, and it is Indigenous conservationists like Sammy Gensaw, Tiana William-Claussen, Secretary Deb Haaland, and members of the Lower Elwha Klallam Tribe who will ensure that wild rivers stay that way—flowing corridors of life that are enriching forests, reconnecting habitats, and sustaining communities.

A NATURE-APPROVED DAM CONSTRUCTION CREW

Breaking (man-made barriers) has been the watchword so far as we conduct our river tours. But we'll now look at a productive, and utterly natural, kind of *making* as we celebrate the role of an industrious, and charming, creature whose structures help rather than hinder riparian wildlife. Beavers are North

America's largest rodents and #1 Ecosystem Engineer. Like the white-lipped peccaries embedding frog-friendly wallows in the Amazon rainforest, beavers reshape and enhance their world. They fashion fabulous 100 percent organic dams that create lush, biodiverse wetlands rather than the nasty tanks of stale water impounded by thick walls of cement.

Wetlands are marshy wildlife havens, thick with aquatic plants. Beaver-engineered wetlands invite and nourish native fish, waterbirds, and insects, along with other semiaquatic mammals. These ponds absorb and slowly release water into a thirsty landscape and filter agricultural runoff (fertilizers, herbicides, and pesticides).

The architectural ingenuity of beaver colonies helps combat some key effects of climate change as well. As the planet heats up and dries out, the swampy, soupy wetlands of beaver country allow water to slowly percolate into the ground, replenishing critical aquifers, or underground springs. These saturated landscapes are also less vulnerable to wildfires. Beaver ponds can even trap carbon from the atmosphere and thus slow climate change itself!

But, you might ask, don't their dams prevent fish from getting where they need to go? Well, unlike solid blocks of cement, the interwoven branches of beaver dams actually permit fish to squeeze through. And beaver-built structures are usually low enough that champion athletes like salmon and trout can leap over them. If all else fails, side channels often flow outward and bypass the dams, allowing fish simply to swim around.

Beaver colonies can also actually help fish, including

salmon, to thrive. Salmon need quiet water and deep pools that allow older fish to rest as they journey upstream and that keep vulnerable fry safe from predators. Beavers can thus serve both generations. The multitudes of insects that swarm and swim in beaver-engineered wetlands provide hearty meals for the fry and light snacks for the big spawners.

Sarah Beesley, Fisheries Biologist of the Yurok Tribe, is using beaver-trademarked techniques as she and her team help the salmon of the Klamath River wait out the demolition of the Iron Gate and its sister dams. Building stream-slowing logjams and "willow log lasagna" dams in the river's tributaries, these biologists are providing fish a kind of off-ramp from the more turbulent main channel. They're also creating prime habitats for native amphibians such as tailed frogs and Dunn's salamanders. "Beavers do it best," says Beesley. But until the gnarly-toothed original ecosystem engineers return to a region where hunters and trappers have wiped them out, the human residents will just have to do *their* best, breaking down giant barriers that sabotage aquatic creatures, and making room for new, watery roads that they can travel.

As ingenious wildlife bridges continue to crisscross the land and newly freed rivers rediscover their ancient, unimpeded channels, another crucial chapter is unfolding in the story of ecological connectivity. This one asks us to read the landscape, and waterways, both with a magnifying glass and a wide-angle lens—to see the minute details of individual wildlife pathways and to glean, more broadly, the sweeping patterns that animals trace as they traverse vast regions unconfined by artificial borders, unfettered by human-made obstacles.

CHAPTER 8
THINKING BIG: WILDLINK CORRIDORS
AND THE FUTURE OF CONNECTIVITY

A narrow overpass spans a sunbaked mountain high-way. The only traffic this bridge has seen in recent years is the occasional tractor or pickup from a local ranch. In the next few years, though, farm equipment may yield right of way to a variety of wildlife. Conservationists, working with the California Department of Transportation, hope to transform this quiet overpass into a busy wildlife crossing.

Though a much more modest structure than the multimillion-dollar bridge inspired by P-22, this Southern California crossing would share a crucial feature with the Liberty Canyon project. Both structures link large swaths of pro-tected land that expand out from either side: wildlife movement corridors that will open up new vistas for mountain lions and other less celebrated species. Without these expansive corridors, crossing structures would just be bridges to nowhere or stray puzzle pieces severed from the bigger conservation picture.

Let's consider how some of the crossings we've visited fit into that larger landscape model of connected habitats and wildlife pathways. Southern California's Harbor Boulevard Wildlife Underpass slots into a 31-mile (50 kilometers) ribbon of canyons, grasslands, and walnut woodlands. This stretch of land connects a huge national forest with a smaller nature reserve. Encircled by freeways, suburbs, and strip malls—a hostile matrix of highly disturbed habitat—the Puente-Chino Hills Wildlife Corridor has become both travel hub and oasis for its native creatures.

In the Kenyan highlands, Tony and his cohort of African elephants duck into an underpass that is just one segment of the 9-mile (14-kilometer) Mount Kenya Elephant Corridor. As they move seasonally between mountain forests and lowland savannahs, the herds are surrounded by wheat and canola fields and ever-expanding villages. Fences separate farms from the corridor—though, as you recall, Tony and other bulls sometimes break through and raid the crops. Still, for the most part, this rural corridor helps the elephant and human communities peacefully coexist and allows once-separated herds to intermingle.

Even the tiny tunnels built for Australia's mountain pygmy possums are part of a contiguous pathway that connects eager males with potential mates awaiting them upslope and on the other side of the Great Alpine Road from the males' habitat. The long strip of boulder fields and loose stones that these intrepid marsupial suiters climb may not make for an easy journey, but both the tunnel underpasses and the larger corridor (several hundred yards/meters) are helping these critically endangered creatures survive habitat loss, climate change, and a relentless stream of automobiles.

Whatever the scale, spacious pachyderm passageway or miniature pygmy possum path, wildlife—*wildlink*—corridors offer the best chance to save the planet's irreplaceable species from the extinction crisis that they're facing.

This last piece of the connectivity puzzle requires more than just resisting the urge to possess and tame the natural world. It asks us to diligently, fiercely protect and even restore the lands and waters that the whole host of wild creatures needs to inhabit and to roam. Identifying and preserving a worldwide web of protected biological corridors and core habitats, we can help ensure that the animals we treasure can keep moving, keep living in the very long run—across distances, and well into the future.

Around the globe, nature lovers are finding lots of ways to create genuine connectivity for mammals, reptiles, amphibians, fish, birds, and insects. **Make, Break, Don't Take** might be their motto, and ours as well. *Make* tunnels and overpasses and canopy crossings for wildlife. *Break* down dams that block the passage of fish and destroy the homes of countless aquatic species. *Don't take* any more of our remaining wildlands or the corridors that connect them. So little is left for us to enjoy, for wildlife to inhabit and traverse. If we can make incredible crossing structures and break at least some of the stubborn dams that block our rivers and streams, we can surely heed the call of *Don't Take*. Don't grab and abuse and destroy what's left of our wild world, our *shared* world.

CONNECTING WILDLIFE ACROSS A CONTINENT: YELLOWSTONE TO YUKON

The fleet pronghorns we witnessed racing across a Wyoming

highway overpass in Chapter 4 helps us see the physical links between individual wildlife crossings and the corridors into which they fit. First we zero in on one node, or point of connection: the bridge itself. Now we step back and view its place within the longer strand that extends 220 miles (355 kilometers): the pronghorn's ancient migratory path. Finally, we zoom out even more and behold a vast network of corridors stretching 1,988 miles (3,200 kilometers) north, from the western United States to the Arctic Circle.

This vista reveals an amazing wildlife superhighway that ecologists, environmentalists, government agencies, and Indigenous communities are working together to preserve with great success. And at its heart is the world's very first national park, Yellowstone, as well as Banff National Park, Canada's first, with the impressive array of wildlife crossings we toured in Chapter 5. The Yellowstone to Yukon Conservation Initiative (Y2Y) has been connecting and protecting habitat and wildlife pathways along the whole sweep of the Rocky Mountains since 1993. Called miistakis, or "Backbone of the World," by the Blackfeet Nation, this rugged range, and the foothills and prairies in its shadow, embraces an incredible population of endangered and threatened species.

Y2Y President and Chief Scientist, Dr. Jodi Hilty, sees the region as a critical stronghold for large animals, including "toothy large carnivores" such as grizzlies, mountain lions, and wolves, as well as sharp-toothed smaller carnivores such as the fierce, fascinating, and elusive wolverine. (You have to love its scientific name: *Gulo gulo*, which means "gluttonous glutton," or perhaps "glutton squared"!) The huge scope of the Y2Y project will be especially important for creatures such as the snow-loving wolverine, likely to need plenty of climate refugia. These are spaces that are relatively protected from the dramatic temperature shifts triggered by climate change. As Dr. Hilty tells me, the diversity of elevations and habitat niches within the Y2Y region can help threatened creatures like the increasingly rare wolverine stay within their ideal "temperature envelope" as climate change permeates the planet. (These envelopes contain the sometimes small range of temperatures that specific creatures need to survive and thrive.)

It was Dr. Hilty's team of conservation biologists that secured a 44-mile (71 kilometers) segment of the Path of the Pronghorn as the United States' first federally designated wildlife corridor. Ensuring safe passage for grizzlies, though, has been at the center of Dr. Hilty's work with Y2Y, whose "transboundary" approach requires working with U.S. and Canadian officials, landowners, and scientists, along with First Nations leaders. Legendary travelers like grizzlies and the surprisingly wide-ranging wolverine know nothing of national, state, or provincial borders. So when Y2Y scientists wanted to reconnect splintered populations of grizzlies through forested corridors, they had to take an international, and interstate, approach. They also had to understand the bears' own movement patterns.

Because *Don't Take*—don't develop, degrade, or destroy—may sometimes mean "purchase to protect," Y2Y raised funds to buy some of the needed land. The organization also relied on conservation easements or covenants, wherein private landowners agree to leave part of their property undeveloped and available to wildlife, often in exchange for tax breaks—or the good feeling you get when helping out planet Earth.

Thanks to purchases, easements, and other protections, the Cabinet-Purcell Mountain Corridor, along with three other linkages, is now running through Montana, Idaho, and British Columbia—shoring up fragmented habitats and helping isolated grizzlies find needed space and one another, across state and national lines. "The way that wildlife sees this landscape is ultimately what matters," Dr. Hilty explains, adding, "We know from the grizzly bear scientists that the bears are now using these corridors."

Farther north into British Columbia, the dynamic duo of grizzlies and salmon are flourishing, as the Y2Y project works to keep waterways such as the Fraser River flowing free. These liquid corridors sustain teeming populations of Chinook, coho, and sockeye salmon. Here, grizzlies and black bears can feast to their heart's content and, in turn, fertilize their forest home with the marine-derived nutrients they disperse.

With their winning combination of ferocity and camera-ready good looks, grizzlies serve as Y2Y's **flagship species.** These are celebrity ambassadors, who like P-22, attract eyes, hearts, and donations. Ursine apex predators also rove the Rockies as Y2Y's most high-profile umbrella species, for their expansive protected habitats, in turn, shelter countless other creatures in the grizzly-centric ecosystem.

Another charismatic carnivore is central to Y2Y's story—its origin story. A female gray wolf, later dubbed Pluie—"rain" in French—was captured in 1991 by a Canadian biologist just south of Banff National Park. He fitted her with a satellite radio collar, the first for a wolf, and released her back into the wild. Her epic journey of two years across two countries ranged over 38,610 square miles (100,000 square kilometers) of nature reserves, public lands, private properties, and Indigenous peoples' territories.

For wildlife biologists, Pluie's travels highlighted just how meaningless human-defined boundaries really are to wild creatures and just how incredibly far they can roam! Another Canadian scientist, Dr. Harvey Locke, took Pluie's lesson to heart and launched the ambitious Yellowstone to Yukon Conservation Initiative, which now enfolds over four hundred partners and expands, year to year, the number of protected areas, corridors, and crossings up and down the Backbone of the World.

The charismatic creatures of the Rocky Mountains are certainly its most glamorous presences. But Dr. Hilty also points to less renowned animals whose smaller, though no less vital, pathways flow into Y2Y's vast network of wildlinks.

Partners like the local volunteers in Alberta's Waterton Lakes National Park are helping long-toed salamanders safely cross the road by building amphibian tunnels similar to those we saw in Amherst, Massachusetts. And another Y2Y partner, British Columbia's Valhalla Wilderness Society, is doing the same for western toads. Protective fencing and a wooden underpass safeguard the adult toads migrating to a nearby lake in March and shield their toadlet offspring as they make the opposite trip in summer.

The truly visionary Yellowstone to Yukon Conservation

Initiative is creating, preserving, and restoring what Dr. Hilty calls "continental-scale connectivity." Yet its scientists and on-the-ground volunteers never lose sight of even the most delicate threads of this grand web of biodiversity, where grizzlies and wolves range within and between huge forests and tiny toadlets hop safely below the road.

TAPIRS AND JAGUARS FIND THEIR WAY IN MESOAMERICA

If toothy large carnivores stalk the spine of the North American continent, Y2Y's key territory, another very different, plant-loving creature snuffles through the rainforests of the Mesoamerican Biological Corridor, which extends 558 miles (900 kilometers) from southern Mexico down to Panama. Though most closely related to rhinos, the bulky Baird's tapir looks like a mash-up of a pig, an elephant, and an anteater, with its barrel-shaped porcine body and trunk-like snout that serves as a snorkel during its daily swim. The largest land animal of the neotropics, the endangered Baird's tapir is called the mountain cow in Belize. But his Columbian handle "macho de monte," or "man of the mountains," better captures his royal status in the biodiversity hotspot where he dwells.

Five feet long and weighing up to 550 pounds (1.5 meters, 250 kilograms), the Baird's tapir is also the great "Gardener of the Forest," a prodigious herbivore who indeed plants new vegetation. Tapirs spread, through their droppings, the seeds of over one hundred plant species, from low shrubs to the large hardwood trees that harbor a huge variety of wildlife *and* suck carbon from the atmosphere. An ecosystem engineer like the bears, beavers, and white-lipped peccaries we've met, the Baird's tapir is also, then, a climate-change warrior, nourishing its forest home. It even rewilds deforested areas. When it wanders from green corridors and national park sanctuaries into the tree-depleted, farm-dominated matrix, it brings the forest back into disturbed and barren lands.

As it fights to protect Baird's tapirs and other threatened species, the Mesoamerican Biological Corridor project, established in 1997, has had less success than that other major transboundary initiative, Y2Y. This is in part because of long-term political tensions, as well as economic pressures to convert wild lands into working cattle ranches and urban spaces. Yet the countries of Belize and Costa Rica offer real bright spots as they preserve and create crucial lifelines—unbroken corridors—between national parks and other wildlife reserves.

The Belize Maya Forest Corridor Trust, for example, is protecting a narrow strip of land that connects two critical regions of the Selva Maya, or Maya Forest. Harboring Baird's tapirs, spider monkeys, and the critically endangered Central American river turtle, this mountainous rainforest also shelters a few squadrons of rare white-lipped peccaries!

Like Y2Y, this coalition relies on close partnerships between government agencies, private landowners, volunteers, and environmental groups such as The Nature Conservancy and Re:Wild. Only 6 miles (10 kilometers) long, the Maya Forest Corridor may seem small, but its role in stitching together patches of the largest tropical rainforest north of the Amazon makes it a true mega-link in the ecological landscape of Mesoamerica.

Another charismatic creature of the region joins the Baird's tapir as a high-profile umbrella species and beneficiary of the Maya Forest pathway. The larger Mesoamerican Biological Corridor project was originally named the Paseo Pantera in its honor. The *pantera*, or jaguar, surpasses even the well-muscled P-22 and his mountain lion kin as the largest, and certainly flashiest, feline in the Americas. And, like mountain lions, these threatened aristocrats need lots of room to roam.

Traveling south from Belize to Costa Rica's Pacific coast, we encounter the spotted big cat in the footage of Central America's largest camera trap study. Combing through nearly fourteen thousand images, wildlife biologists and local citizen scientists witnessed tapirs and peccaries, ocelots and crab-eating raccoons, armadillos, and weasel-like greater grisons—the "South American wolverine." All these creatures were photographed roaming the lush Osa Peninsula's two main national parks and their connective corridors. As biologists like the study's lead author Dr. Juan Sebastián Vargas Soto investigated the role and (wildlife) traffic flow of the linkages, it was jaguars that offered some of the best clues.

"Using unique spot patterns to distinguish individuals," Dr. Vargas Soto informs me, researchers could track how several specific jaguars were moving through the park and corridors, and at times straying into unprotected areas. Clearly identified individual cats confirm to scientists that it's not just the same animal taking multiple selfies! While the Osa Biological Corridor is the main artery between the peninsula's two national parks, this in-depth study of the region exposed the need for even more linkages that will allow tapirs, jaguars, and maybe even a few white-lipped peccaries to steer clear of the palm oil and teak plantations and the towns and roads scattered across the Osa Peninsula.

Groups like Osa Conservation are expanding the corridor network by buying up land and negotiating easements with local landowners, as well as launching their own camera trap studies to find the best places for wildlife crossings. The good news, as Dr. Vargas Soto confirms, is that specialist species like jaguars, tapirs, and grisons, and their more common neighbors such as hog-nosed skunks and red brocket deer, are indeed traversing the corridors.

Key puzzle pieces like the linkages in Belize and Costa Rica help bring the broader connectivity picture envisioned by the Mesoamerican Biological Corridor into sharper focus, and closer to reality. And these wildlinks, mega or seemingly more modest, enable Baird's tapirs to continue their vital work as Gardeners of the Forests and invite jaguars to prowl broader tracts of wilderness, moving silently through a land that is, in turn, moving toward wholeness.

TIGERSCAPES IN THE KINGDOM OF BHUTAN

Wedged between two giants, China and India, and perched on the world's highest mountain range, Bhutan is a tiny country with big cats and an even bigger commitment to the natural world. Though smaller than Costa Rica, and about half the size of Texas, this Southeast Asian kingdom is a global giant in terms of its epic Bhutan Biological Conservation

Complex (B2C2). This title refers to the network of protected lands themselves: national parks and wildlife sanctuaries and biological corridors. But it also represents the project's guiding principle: "Living in Harmony with Nature."

Bhutan takes its role as steward of the Eastern Himalayan biodiversity hotspot extremely seriously. Hunting is illegal, and the country's constitution, in fact, mandates that 60 percent of its land remain forested. With over 70 percent of the nation covered in pines, oaks, magnolias, and bamboo, Bhutan joins Costa Rica as one of just a handful of countries to actually *reverse* deforestation! In 2018, the densely wooded Bhutan became the world's first carbon sink, a nation that absorbs more carbon than it emits and thus helps offset global warming.

Champion defender of wildlife habitat and fierce foe of climate change, Bhutan is showing the rest of the world how to think big and act decisively. 30 by 30 (30 x 30) is a catchphrase that scientists, conservationists, and progressive politicians throughout the globe are currently circulating. We must, they argue, protect 30 percent of the world's lands, freshwaters, and oceans by 2030 to stave off massive extinctions and calamitous climate change. Biologist Dr. Edward O. Wilson boosted that percentage to 50 in his Half-Earth Project.

Well, Bhutan has already protected *more* than 50 percent of its ecologically diverse territory! Specifically designated linkages are a huge part of its B2C2 program. 1999 provided a remarkable chapter in the story of habitat connectivity, when, as a "Gift to the Earth from the People of Bhutan," the nation bestowed twelve specific, formally named biological corridors.

Flowing between a number of major protected sites, these corridors comprise an unprecedented 10 percent of Bhutan's total area.

And together, Bhutan's cores and corridors—its wildlife sanctuaries and wildlinks web—safeguard and connect an amazing variety of wildlife. Malayan giant squirrels dash across treetops in the broadleaf forest. Exquisite black-necked cranes winter in valley wetlands. Red pandas or "firefoxes"—just don't call them "lesser pandas"!—munch on bamboo in the Black Mountains, while the shaggy takin, with a broad moose-like nose and bovine body, heaves its massive bulk up steep alpine slopes. Families of Asian elephants lumber through Bhutan's three elephant crossings carved beneath a wide motorway. Troops of gleaming golden langurs, among the world's twenty-five most endangered primates, seek sweet fruits high in the forest canopy. Looking closer, in the branches or on the ground, we discover a macabre assemblage of arachnids: goblin spiders, monkey spiders, wolf spiders, and, most alarmingly, jumping spiders.

But perhaps it's Bhutan's resident felines who best capture our imaginations and conjure nature's most sublime magic. Dizzying altitudes and freezing temperatures don't discourage the almost mythical snow leopard. With giant paws that firmly grip slippery rocks and provide "snowshoes" in the deepest winter drifts, the "Ghost of the Mountains" is among the world's most elusive animals. The fact that it dines on bharal, or blue sheep, only adds to its storybook mystique.

While snow leopards, in their rugged Himalayan heights, remain nearly invisible, the equally rare, equally magnifcent

Bengal tiger is helping wildlife biologists solve Bhutan's conservation and connectivity puzzles as it strolls through extensive camera trap footage. With distinctive stripes, like the unique spots of Costa Rica's jaguars, individual tigers in the still photos and dramatic videos of Bhutan's first National Tiger Census (2014–2015) showed wildlife biologists that the world's largest felines are indeed finding safe passage through the conserved linkages.

Dr. Tshering Tempa, Bhutan's leading tiger biologist and advocate is also tracking tigers through radio collar data. The country's first radio-collared tiger, a young female dubbed Tendrel Zangmo, or "Auspicious Omen," is showing Dr. Tempa and his team how she and other tigers are moving through the officially designated corridors. These tigers are also helping scientists identify new routes that may need protection.

One of just thirteen countries where tigers still roam, Bhutan embraces what Dr. Tempa calls globally significant "tigerscapes," areas where these endangered apex predators are already flourishing and reproducing. Tigerscapes also refer to future habitats replete with favorite prey like sambar deer and wild pigs and that are thus ready for the big cats to colonize.

As a vital link between the tigers of Myanmar and of northeast India, Bhutan has not only gifted the Earth important wildlife corridors within its borders—it is *itself* actually a wild-link. This small country offers the kind of transnational connectivity also central to the Y2Y and Mesoamerican projects. Tigers are an umbrella species, like the elephants of Mount Kenya, the mountain lions of Southern California, the grizzlies of Canada, and the jaguars and tapirs of Central America.

Thus Bhutan's Bengal tigers open the way for countless other creatures as they cross national borders or dwell within a more narrow home range, perhaps in the frozen alpine peaks or subtropical lowlands of this Himalayan wildlife stronghold.

WILDLIFE ON THE FARM

In a mosaic of Costa Rican rainforest and farmland, one citrus grower named Adonis wanted to help the local Baird's tapirs struggling to survive in their severely fragmented habitat. He allowed the forest to creep back into a section of his land once covered with tangerine groves, inviting numerous tapirs, who, in turn, helped plant more native trees and shrubs when they deposited seeds foraged in the adjoining old-growth forest. Together, this eco-friendly farmer and the Gardener of the Forest are rewilding the land, creating new wildlife habitat and pathways, and proving that smaller wildlinks can, and must, join the grander corridor projects unfolding in Central America, Bhutan, and the Yellowstone to Yukon region.

An unusual farm in Southern California also balances agriculture with wildlife-friendly practices, welcoming native creatures from gopher snakes to great horned owls. Starring in the documentary *The Biggest Little Farm* (2018), directed by owner John Chester, Apricot Lane Farms is a biodynamic farm, which means that Chester and his wife, Molly, see their land as a living organism, an intact, biodiverse ecosystem that both produces crops and supports native plants and wildlife.

When I spend a morning on the farm with Ruby Molinari, who leads its Habitat Restoration program, and her colleague Lucas Carlow, they first show me the various wildlife movement corridors that weave through the property. Most crucial are barrancas, steep-sided ravines etched into the ground by seasonal rivers and streams. Lined with willows and cotton-woods, these barrancas invite such travelers as badgers, bobcats, rabbits, raccoons, and coyotes. The coyote den that Molinari points out to me confirms that, for some local wildlife, Apricot Lane Farms is a home and not just a transit route.

Native plants provide the foundation for all wildlife habitats and pathways, and Molinari's Habitat Restoration team has brought the farm's original number of native plant species from 60 up to 250. Molinari later tells me, "We try to orchestrate successive blooming periods, and a variety of plants and flower shapes provides for various kind of pollinators."

She and Carlow show me other wildlife-friendly features. Gnarled apple and apricot trees not part of the official orchards drop their knobby fruit for birds and animals. Piles of sticks left intact for lizards and mice to crawl under resemble the rustic faunal furniture installed on green bridges throughout the world, welcoming and reassuring wild travelers.

The farm's willow-lined barrancas and oak-ringed pond, where ducklings paddle and a snowy egret dips its long bill, remind me that shade and water are just what resident and visiting wildlife will need more of as climate change takes its toll. Apricot Lane Farms may indeed become a climate refuge for wildlife needing a haven from the heat here in drought-stricken California.

A few days after my visit, Molinari sends me a message that really sums up what it means to farm, and maybe even to live, in an ecologically responsible way: "If we are going to be farming this land, we need to provide the space for the wildlife to coexist. We are in their space and we owe it to them to include and honor them in our land use practices. It looks and feels good to be farming in this way. A farm without wildlife is a fabricated system." With the help of Molinari, Carlow, and the whole Habitat Restoration team, the biggest little farm has become a vital wildlink for creatures on the move or wanting to settle in for a longer stay.

STEPPING STONES AND STOPOVERS FOR WINGED TRAVELERS

During my visit to the farm, Carlow, Molinari, and I walk past a long row of clumpy bushes with dark-green leaves and open-faced magenta blossoms. Spaced a few feet apart, these California wild roses benefit one of the farm's most adorable visitors: California quail. Plump and squat, this compact bundle of feathers sports a comma-shaped plume that droops over its forehead like a tiny visor. Its stubby wings make for poor flying skills, so quail are ground dwellers and need lots of protective cover as they go about their business of foraging and evading predators.

As they race from bush to bush, quail use the plants as **stepping stone corridors**, paths that are broken into segments but still effective. Close together and with clear sight lines between them, the intermittent points of refuge that the wild roses and other native shrubs provide make these timid birds feel right at home.

When we circle back to the pond and the waterbirds we see there, our talk turns from the quail's modest cluster of terrestrial stepping stones to the connectivity needs of migratory birds.

Marathon fliers likes Canada geese, kingfishers, and egrets, who cross whole continents, need to touch down periodically in order to rest and refuel. Conservationists around the world are protecting, and even creating, these crucial **stopover sites**, safe temporary havens for wanderers on the wing.

A Bird Airport in Northern China

A truly innovative avian connectivity project is unfolding in a Chinese port city: the world's first "bird airport." Still under construction, Tianjin's Lingang Bird Sanctuary will be a refuge for resident wildlife, particularly shorebirds, and a stopover and breeding site for the fifty million birds that stream south from the Arctic. The city of Tianjin is located along a major **flyway**, a seasonal flight path of migratory birds. The East Asian-Australasian Flyway flows from Siberia and Alaska in the north down to Australia and New Zealand in the south. Already hosting many long-distance travelers even in its unfinished state, the sanctuary will be a 150-acre (61-hectare) park and wetlands that will give a smog-choked city "new green lungs," along with an education and research center for human visitors.

In terms of **Make, Break, Don't Take**, Tianjin's wildlife connectivity hub blends all three. First, planners had to demolish (break) a giant waste disposal facility. Then leaders of this crowded city, among China's ten most populous, had to decide not to scoop up (take) the land for even more housing and commercial development. Finally, Tianjin's public officials, conservationists, landscape architects, and citizens had to cooperate in funding, designing, and creating (making) a world-class wildlife refuge. The bird airport will feature an island lake, reedy lagoons, and nutrient-rich mudflats.

Global migrators along the East Asian–Australasian Flyway, like black-tailed godwits, the national bird of the Netherlands, and yellow bitterns, who love to poke along the reeds in search of small fish, will certainly include the Lingang Bird Sanctuary in their itineraries as a premier rest, nest, and refuel site. From landfill to lush wetlands, this urban refuge definitely takes rewilding to an impressive new level.

Pollinators, Songbirds, and Shorebirds Touch Down in New York City

Another megacity, this one in the U.S., offers a wide variety of accommodations and stepping stone pathways for shorebirds and other avian migrators, as well as for the millions of pollinators—birds, bees, bats, and butterflies—that power the urban ecosystem. And yes, cities do enfold ecosystems! You can find "nearby nature" in pocket parks and backyards, potted plants on your stoop, and strips of native flowers and foliage like those that file along sidewalks. Although these spaces may seem small or insignificant, they provide vital stopover sites and pathways just like the larger-scale Lingang Bird Sanctuary.

New York City is where we'll conclude our tour of stepping stone corridors. Dr. Dustin Partridge, the aptly named Director of Conservation and Science at NYC Audubon, tells me of four prime stopover habitats that help both resident and migratory winged creatures find their way through a concrete jungle that actually includes a lot of green space.

First, within the famed 843 acres (341 hectares) of Manhattan's Central Park, you can find the Ramble, an actual forest where songbirds like warblers find safe haven in the spring and cedar waxwings take a break from their autumn journey. Raptors—birds of prey—such as screech owls and red-tailed hawks also find the densely wooded Ramble a good place to roost and hunt. Native oaks are keystone members of this urban forest, hosting dozens of caterpillar species and other insects that provide rich meals for famished travelers and foraging residents.

We'll now briefly touch down on two dramatically rewilded sites in New York City that are attracting, and providing safe passage for, pollinators and songbirds year-round.

On Manhattan's West Side, a foliage-covered former elevated freight-rail line weaves a green thread through a once heavily industrial zone. Two stories above the street, the High Line gardens attract butterflies, moths, dragonflies, and spiders, as well as thirty species of wild bees. Orioles and woodpeckers, kinglets and mockingbirds find an excellent travel route along this plant-draped rail line, too. Clusters of tricolor crocus, yellow dogtooth violets, and black chokeberry, among other native flowering plants, have transformed these train tracks into a very different thoroughfare.

Moving to the borough of Brooklyn, we discover another industrial space turned wild. Kingsland Wildflowers Green Roof & Community Engagement Center invites us to wander atop a movie studio next to a noisy recycling facility. Flowering plants

and native grasses have transformed this roof into an island of calm that somehow quiets even the clamor of the machinery and traffic. As we cross the rooftop garden on actual stepping stones embedded in meadows of purple aster, we realize that this green roof, one of many in New York and other cities, provides a stepping stone corridor for pollinators like swallowtail butterflies, migratory eastern red bats, and ruby-throated hummingbirds. Phoebes and flycatchers snatch the flies and midges that hover around the foliage of this botanical oasis.

After climbing up to the West Side's elevated rail and the Brooklyn rooftop, we come back down to earth, and sea, as we return to our shorebird theme. With dozens of small islands and lush saltmarshes, the Jamaica Bay Wildlife Refuge in Queens is a paradise for the migrating herons, egrets, and snow geese who flock here every spring to gorge on horseshoe crab eggs. Dr. Partridge speaks fondly of his own favorite Jamaica Bay visitor, the red knot. Ordinarily a somewhat nondescript fellow with dull gray plumage, this medium-size shorebird arrives in his Arctic breeding grounds ready to impress with the shimmering reds and golds of his mating-season finery. Flying an astonishing 18,000-mile round trip (29,000 kilometers) from the far north to his Tierra del Fuego winter residence, the intrepid red knot definitely needs the high-calorie crab eggs he finds in Queens to carry him through his epic journey!

The Jamaica Bay Wildlife Refuge highlights the critical role of urban green—and watery blue—space for the winged migrators, whose vast corridors in the sky still need wildlink networks below, on land and water, to help these marvelous navigators complete their travels.

A FREER PATH THROUGH
LIBERTY CANYON

It's early morning on Earth Day, and I'm back at Liberty Canyon. This time I'm on the opposite side of the freeway, walking up the same hills upon which I'd gazed the summer before. The slopes are now green, not the soft browns and grays of July, and a light rain has left them shimmering and fragrant. A lone flame-charred oak stands sentinel nearby, survivor of a ferocious wildfire four years earlier. While fluffy clouds cast moving shadows on steep ravines, I watch a turkey vulture stretch its huge wings as it floats effortlessly over the freeway.

Amidst all this natural beauty, a very different scene is unfolding. At least twenty vans from local and national media outlets have parked in the canyon's access road, and reporters with mikes and bulky cameras are beginning to swarm the scene. Folks in hiking boots and T-shirts proclaiming #SaveLACougars and P-22 Is My Homeboy traipse toward a large white tent. The atmosphere is festive, like a carnival or, more fittingly for this Hollywood-adjacent locale, a movie premiere. A volunteer from the National Wildlife Federation lugs a bulky cardboard P-22 up the hill. It's clear who the star of the day is, and I'll later join the line of P-22 fans eager to nab a photo with his remarkably lifelike stand-in.

After decades of scientific research, fundraising, and public awareness campaigns featuring P-22, the day to break ground for the Wallis Annenberg Wildlife Crossing is finally here, and I'm one of the lucky guests given a green wristband and access to the event.

Chumash and Tataviam elder Alan Salazar opens the

ceremony with a blessing. He burns sage in a small bowl and acknowledges this hillside as the homeland of his people, who have always shared it with the mountain lions and lizards and white-shouldered hawks. "We need them more than they need us," he observes, then gestures to the freeway behind him: "But it's our job to protect them." Beth Pratt, Miguel Ordeñana, Jeff Sikich, and many others speak movingly about the project and the big cat who helped make it possible.

The head of the project's design team, Robert Rock from Living Habitats, recalls his father's advice: "Leave a place better than you found it." Liberty Canyon, where an impassable freeway seemed to spell doom for the wildlife on either side, will indeed be a better place, finally living up to its name as a new path to freedom reaches across ten lanes of ever-flowing traffic.

When the ceremony nears its close, the crossing's generous benefactor, philanthropist Wallis Annenberg, tells us, "We can begin to make the land whole again for all. We can share this earth instead of claiming it and dominating it. We can coexist side by side." Here are two key facets of our **Make, Break, Don't Take** motto for wildlife corridors, crossings, and, we can add, coexistence. We will, together, make the Earth whole. We will refrain from claiming, or taking, the land for our own sole purposes. A bit later, when the bridge's namesake joins Pratt and other conservation heroes outside the tent, the final term slides into place. With reporters snapping pictures, golden shovels break the ground, opening a new path for Los Angeles's mountain lions, and giving hope to wild creatures around the world. P-22 would be proud.

EPILOGUE

Eight months after the Wallis Annenberg Wildlife Crossing broke ground, the bridge's greatest inspiration and Los Angeles's most beloved wild animal was gone. At twelve years of age, an astonishingly long life for a mountain lion, P-22 passed away, having prowled his Griffith Park kingdom for ten years. Some of the magic in the Hollywood Hills disappeared that day, even as heartfelt tributes poured in from around the world.

Yet P-22's legacy is secure, engraved in our hearts, and grafted onto the green bridge that will allow his fellow cougars once again to range freely through the land they once proudly ruled. More such crossings and corridors are sure to spring up in his memory, opening paths for mountain lions and other native wildlife well past the borders of P-22's Southern California domain. The ghost cat has become an abiding spirit, galvanizing our ongoing quest to protect, and connect, the remarkable wild creatures with whom we share this planet.

And just four days before P-22 died, the National Parks

Service announced the recent birth of four cougar kittens in the Santa Monica Mountains. As the bridge that is rising from P-22's legendary life moves closer to completion, it will beckon P-109, P-110, P-111, and P-112 to venture forth on their own epic journeys, striding high above the roadway, toward the vast wildlands beyond.

A VITAL LINK TO NATURE: YOU!

From Beth Pratt in Southern California to Robin Petersen in South Africa, we've met lots of people who are making sure that wildlife can move safely through the world we all share. But you don't have to raise $90 million for the world's biggest wildlife bridge or work in a giant national park to be an eco-hero!

Here are a few ways to help wild creatures, and the whole natural world. Just be sure to get permission from your parents before exploring any online resources!

Check out the free National Geographic–approved *Seek* app that allows you to identify species, collect data, and earn badges for finding specific plants, insects, and more.
https://media.nationalgeographic.org/assets/file/Seek _Pocket_Guide-One-pager-FINAL_1.pdf?_gl=1*1rezcfv*_ga*MTUON k1ODg3Ni4xNjU2MTkxMDg1*_ga_JRRKGYJRKE*MTY1NjE5M TA4NS4xLjAuMTY1NjE5MTA4NS4w

Become a citizen scientist by signing up with National Geographic's *iNaturalist*. As its website declares, "Every observation can contribute to biodiversity science, from the rarest butterfly to the most common backyard weed. We share your findings with scientific data repositories . . . to help scientists to find and use your data. All you have to do is observe." https://www.inaturalist.org/

Participate in or organize a *BioBlitz*, a high-octane scavenger hunt for native species in a particular area and in a short time.
https://www.nationalgeographic.org/projects/bioblitz/

Join the University of Wisconsin-based website *JourneyNorth*, which tracks wildlife migrations of all kinds, including monarch but-terflies and songbirds. Here's another opportunity for you to become a citizen scientist and report sightings all year round.

https://journeynorth.org/

Start a wildlife-friendly garden at your school. *The National Wildlife Federation Schoolyard Habitat* program can help you, your classmates, and your teachers create something really special!

https://www.nwf.org/Garden-for-Wildlife/Create/Schoolyards

Plant a *Pollinator Pathway* in your neighborhood. Here's the official toolkit to get you started.

http://pollinatorpathways.com/wp-content/uploads/2021/07/POLLINATOR-PATHWAY-TOOLKIT.pdf.

In order to identify roadkill hotspots, scientists at the Road Ecology Center (University of California, Davis) and the The Road Lab (formerly Project Splatter—yikes!) in the UK have developed apps for documenting animals hit by cars. You, too, can become a Road-kill Warrior and help wildlife avoid this grisly fate; the data you send will help wildlife biologists, road ecologists, and transportation agen-cies understand where to lower speed limits, put up warning signs (TURTLE X-ING! WATCH OUT FOR WALLABIES!), and maybe even build a wildlife bridge. Here's the info for UC Davis's California Roadkill Observation System (CROS). Please work closely with an adult if you decide to mon-itor roadkill! https://roadecology.ucdavis.edu/research/projects/cros

Stay curious, stay connected, stay compassionate!

SCIENTIFIC NAMES OF SELECT SPECIES

~~~~~~~~~~~~~~~

For the most part, we've been using animals' common names through-out the book, but these labels can vary depending on region—and language. They can also multiply because, well, it's fun to invent names! For more precision, when scientists refer to plants and animals, they use what's called their "Latin binomials," a universal system of double names, the first being the genus, or larger community of organisms, and the second a specific descriptor. Hence, though P-22 may have liked us to call him (at least in English) a cougar, mountain lion, or puma, biologists prefer *Puma concolor*, or uniformly colored puma.

Common name, *scientific name*
(in the order that they appear in the book)

Chapter 1

mountain lion, *Puma concolor*
North American beaver, *Castor canadensis*
koala, *Phascolarctos cinereus*
western spadefoot toad, *Spea hammondii*
Arctic tern, *Sterna paradisaea*

Chapter 2

Galápagos giant tortoise, *Chelonoidis niger*
white-lipped peccary, *Tayassu pecari*
giant monkey frog, *Phyllomedusa bicolor*
tiger-striped leaf frog, *Phyllomedusa tomopterna*

Chapter 3

Timema walking stick, *Timema cristinae*
pallid bat, *Antrozous pallidus*

Chapter 4

weaver ant, *Oecophylla smaragdina*
leaf-cutting ant, *Atta cephalotes*
    (just one of many varieties)
Pacific banana slug, *Ariolimax columbianus*
Roosevelt elk, *Cervus canadensis roosevelti*
    (this one's a trinomial!)
spotted salamander, *Ambystoma maculatum*
mountain pygmy possum, *Burramys parvus*
African bush elephant, *Loxodonta africana*
Quino checkerspot butterfly, *Euphydryas editha*
    quino (another trinomial)
pronghorn, *Antilocapra americana*
golden lion tamarin, *Leontopithecus rosalia*
lion-tailed macaque, *Macaca silenus*
bobcat, *Lynx rufus*
coyote, *Canis latrans*
mule deer, *Odocoileus hemionus*

Chapter 5

common wombat, *Vombatus ursinus*
sugar glider, *Petaurus breviceps*
Sunda pangolin, *Manis javanca*
Asian palm civet, *Paradoxurus hermaphroditus*
sambar deer, *Rusa unicolor*
roe deer, *Capreolus capreolus*
European badger, *Meles meles*
European pine marten, *Martes martes*
grizzly bear, *Ursus arctos horribilis*
bighorn sheep, *Ovis canadensis*
black bear, *Ursus americanus*
Canada goose, *Branta canadensis*

Chapter 7

Southern California steelhead,
   Oncorhynchus mykiss
Chinook salmon (king salmon),
   Oncorhynchus tshawytscha
sockeye salmon, *Oncorhynchus nerka*
African tiger fish, *Hydrocynus vittatus*
African fish eagle, *Haliaeetus vocifer*
African longfin eel, *Anguilla mossambica*
African mottled eel, *Anguilla bengalensis*
ayu (sweetfish), *Plecoglossus altivelis*
Blakiston's fish owl, *Bubo blakistoni*
white-spotted char (Japanese *ame masu*,
"rain salmon"), *Salvelinus leucomaenis*
Dolly Varden char, *Salvelinus malma*
Steller's sea eagle, *Haliaeetus pelagicus*
Ussuri brown bear, *Ursus arctos lasiotus*
California condor (Yurok *prey-go-neesh*), *Gymnogyps*
   californianus

Chapter 8

wolverine, *Gulo gulo*
gray wolf, *Canis lupus*
long-toed salamander, *Ambystoma macrodactylum*
western toad, *Anaxyrus boreas*
Baird's tapir (Spanish *macho de monte*, "man
   of the mountains"), *Tapirus bairdii*
jaguar (Spanish *pantera*), *Panthera onca*
red panda (firefox), *Ailurus fulgens*
takin (gnu goat), *Budorcas taxicolor*
Asian elephant, *Elephas maximus*
snow leopard, *Panthera uncia*

blue sheep (bharal), *Psuedois nayaur*
Bengal tiger, *Panthera tigris tigris*
California quail, *Callipepla californica*
black-tailed godwit, *Limosa limosa*
eastern red bat, *Lasiurus borealis*
red knot, *Calidris canutus*

BIBLIOGRAPHY

Abson, Rodney. "The use by vertebrate fauna of the Slaty Creek Wildlife Underpass, Calder Freeway, Black Forest, Macedon, Victoria." Master's Thesis, University of Tasmania. 2004.

Abson, Rodney N. and Ruth E. Lawrence. "Monitoring the use of the Slaty Creek Wildlife Underpass, Calder Freeway, Black Forest, Macedon, Victoria, Australia." Procedings of the ICOET (International Conference on Ecology & Transportation). Lake Placid, New York. August 2003.

Anderson, Mark. "Saving the Future for Biodiversity: Finding and protecting the most climate-resilient places—and the paths species will take to get there." The Nature Conservancy. Website. 6 February 2023. https://www.nature.org/en-us/what-we-do/our-insights /perspectives/saving-future-stage-biodiversity-mark-anderson /. Accessed 28 April 2023.

Apricot Lane Farms. Website. https://www.apricotlanefarms .com/. Accessed 22 June 2022.

Ascensão, Fernando, et al. "Roads, traffic and verges: Big problems and big opportunities for small mammals." *Handbook of Road Ecology*. Eds. Rodney van der Ree, et al. Chichester, West Sussex: Wiley Blackwell, 2015. 325–333.

Beck, Harald, et al. "Do Neotropical peccary species (Tayassuidae) function as ecosystem engineers for anurans?" *Journal of Tropical Ecology* 26 (2010): 407–414.

Beesley, Sarah. "Yurok Tribal Fisheries Restoration and Protection in the Lower Klamath." Salmonid Restoration Federation Conference. 13 March 2015. https://vimeo.com/132852003. Accessed 14 June 2022.

Bhutan Biological Conservation Complex: Living in Harmony with the Nature. A Landscape Conservation Plan: A Way Forward. Nature Conservation Division, Department of Forestry Services, Ministry of Agriculture, with support from WWF Bhutan. 2004.

Borrell, Brendan. "Saving the Maya Rainforest." *Nature Conservancy* (Winter 2021): 51–59.

Chen, Maxine. "How effective are wildlife corridors like Singapore's Eco-Link?" *Mongabay: News & Inspiration from Nature's Frontline.* 26 July 2017. https://news.mongabay.com/2017/07/how-effective-are-wildlife-corridors-like-singapores-eco-link/. Accessed 22 March 2022.

Choo, Daryl. "Mandai wildlife bridge: Rare sambar deer among nearly 70 species spotted using crossing." *Today.* 3 February 2022. https://www.todayonline.com/singapore/mandai-wildlife-bridge -rare-sambar-deer-among-nearly-70-species-spotted-using-cross ing-1808361. Accessed 22 March 2022.

Cooke, Lucy. "Gardeners of the Forest." *BBC Wildlife* (April 2022): 56–65.

Crossings Amid Climate Change: Reconnecting California's Landscapes. Secretary Speaker Series. California Natural Resources Agency. 21 March 2022. https://www.youtube.com/watch?v=4N M7i8Xq1Es&t=2023s. Accessed 8 June 2022.

Daly, Christopher B. "For Salamanders, The 'Big Night' Is Everything." *The Washington Post.* 18 April 1993. https://www.washing tonpost.com/archive/politics/1993/04/18/for-salamanders-the-big -night-is-everything/42bdff5e-52e6-41e6-b995-d48b6787b9c0 / Accessed 16 March 2022.

de Souza, Marcelo and Mario Lobao. "Endangered Brazilian monkeys get a bridge to themselves." *The Washington Post.* 7 August 2020. https://apnews.com/article/brazil-rio-de-janeiro-ap-top-news-an imals-forests-00bcb9de4f5ee871e504ef50c5b6d06a. Accessed 19 March 2022.

Dickie, Gloria. "As Banff's famed wildlife overpasses turn 20, the world looks to Canada for conservation inspiration." *Canadian Geographic.* 4 December 2017. https://www.canadiangeographic.ca /article/banffs-famed-wildlife-overpasses-turn-20-world-looks-can /ada-conservation-inspiration. Accessed 25 March 2022.

Endangered Species Act of 1973: As Amended through the 108th Congress. Department of the Interior and U.S. Fish and Wildlife Service. https://www.fws.gov/sites/default/files/documents/endan gered -species-act-accessible_6.pdf Accessed December 17 2021.

Farji-Brener, Alejandro G., et al. "Fallen Branches as Part of Leaf-Cutting Ant Trails: Their Role in Resource Discovery and Leaf Transport Rates in *Atta cephalotes.*" *Biotropica* 39: March 2007. https://www.jstor.org/stable/30045395?sid=primo#metadata_info _tab_contents. Accessed 28 August 2022.

"First Dam Removal in Japan." Dam Removal Europe. 12 January 2018. Website. https://damremoval.eu/ 日本における最初のダム撤去-yes-you-understood-correctly-first-dam-removal-in-japan/Accessed 5 May 2023.

Forman, Richard T. T., et al. *Road Ecology: Science and Solutions.* Washington/Covelo/London: Island Press, 2003.

Free Rivers: The State of Dam Removal in the United States. February 2022. American Rivers. Website. https://www.americanrivers. org/wcontent/uploads/2022/02/DamList2021_Report_02172022 _FINAL3.pdf. Accessed 7 June 2022.

Fuchs, Hannah. "China builds first bird airport." *DW*. 3 March 2017. https://www.dw.com/en/china-builds-first-bird-airport-to-attract -feathered-friends/a-37795569. Accessed 24 June 2022.

Ghazoul, Jaboury. *Ecology: A Very Short Introduction.* Oxford: Oxford UP, 2020.

Gibbens, Sarah. "World's Happiest Country Also Has No Carbon Emissions." *National Geographic.* 7 July 2018. https://www.national geographic.co.uk/perpetual-planet/2018/07/worlds-happiest-coun try-also-has-no-carbon-emissions. Accessed 21 June 2022.

Goldfarb, Ben. "Ecosystem Engineer." *Sierra.* July/August 2018: 34–35.

"Grand Canyon: No Bullets Through the Heart." *Sierra.* September /October 1993: 62–63.

Gupta, Trisha. "Lion-tailed Macaque: Acrobats of the Upper

Canopy." *Roundglass/Sustain*. 13 May 2022. https://sustain.round.glass/species/lion-tailed-macaque-western-ghats/. Accessed 20 July 2022.

Haaland, Deb (United States Secretary of the Interior). Letter to Kimberly D. Bose, Secretary, Federal Energy Regulatory Commission. *North Coast Journal*. 10 June 2021. https://p.northcoastjournal.com/media/pdf/20210611-5056_secretary_letter_to_ferc_06-10-2021.pdf. Accessed 5 April 2023.

Hall, Len and Rodney Abson. "Calder Freeway Wildlife Crossings." 22nd ARRB Conference—Research into Practice. Canberra Australia, 2006.

Hance, Jeremy. "How the overlooked peccary engineers the Amazon, an interview with Harald Beck." *Mongabay: News & Inspiration from Nature's Frontline*. 20 September 2010. https://news.mongabay.com/2010/09/how-the-overlooked-peccary-engineers-the-amazon-an-interview-with-harald-beck/. Accessed 15 December 2021.

"Harbor Boulevard Wildlife Underpass: First in Los Angeles County." Puente Hills Habitat Preservation Authority. Website. https://www.habitatauthority.org/harbor-boulevard-wildlife-underpass/. Accessed 26 March 2022.

"Henry Street Salamander Tunnels." Hitchcock Center: Education for a Healthy Planet. Website. https://www.hitchcockcenter.org/programs/henry-street-salamander-tunnels/. Accessed 1 March 2022.

Hilty, Jodi A. "Y2Y: A Model for Large-Scale Connectivity." Connecting People Who Connect Wildlife: Crossings, Corridors, and More! Symposium at the 69th Annual Meeting of the Western Section of the Wildlife Society. 7 February 2022.

Hilty, Jodi A., et al. *Corridor Ecology: Linking Landscapes for Biodiversity Conservation and Climate Adaptation*. 2nd ed. Washington/Covelo/London: Island Press, 2019.

"How Did the Grizzly Bear Cross the Road?" (video). *Parks Canada: Exploring By the Seat of Your Pants*. 17 November 2021. https://www.youtube.com/watch?v=f1sWagkqHnE. Accessed 1 April 2022.

Iinuma, Sayoko. "Removal of the Arase Dam: Japan's First

Attempt to Dismantle a Hydroelectric Dam and Restore the Original River Environment." *Nature and Our Future: The Mekong Basin and Japan*, eds. Toshiyuki Doi and Madoka Chase Onizuka. Mitsui & Co., Ltd. Environment Fund: 2013. 1–5. http://www.mekongwatch.org/plat form/bp/english4-2.pdf. Accessed 4 May 2023.

Kahn, Jo. "Decline in bogong moth numbers could have cata-strophic effects in the Australian Alps." ABC Science News. Australian Broadcasting Corporation. 26 February 2019. https://www.abc.net .au/news/science/2019-02-27/bogong-moth-decline-in-australian -alps/10850036. Accessed 17 March 2022.

Kay, Elma. "Protecting the Maya Forest Corridor." Re:Wild. Website. https://www.rewild.org/wild-about/maya-forest-corridor. Accessed 18 June 2022.

"Keeping toads off roads." 13 March 2020. Yellowstone to Yukon Conservation Initiative. Website. https://y2y.net/blog/keeping-toads -off-roads/. Accessed 17 June 2022.

Kelleher, Shannon. "How wildlife crossings in Canada are inspir-ing safer roads for global species." *Mongabay: News & Inspiration from Nature's Frontline*. 17 December 2021. https://news.mongabay .com/2021/12/how-wildlife-crossings-in-canada-are-inspiring-safer -roads-for-global-species/. Accessed 25 March 2022.

Khamcha, Daphawan, et al. "Road induced edge effects on a for-est bird community in tropical Asia." *Avian Research* (2018). https:// digitalcommons.unl.edu/cgi/viewcontent.cgi?article=1816&context =natrespapers. Accessed 1 April 2022.

"Klamath Dam Removal Process Enters Home Stretch." Press Release. 25 February 2022. The Yurok Tribe. Website. https://www .yuroktribe.org/post/press-release-klamath-dam-removal-process -enters-home-stretch. Accessed 13 June 2022.

Kolbert, Elizabeth. The Sixth Extinction: An Unnatural History. New York: Picador, 2014.

Koshino, Yosuke, Hideaki Kudo, and Masahide Kaeriyama. "Sta-ble isotope evidence indicates the incorporation into Japanese catchments of marine-derived nutrients transported by spawning Pacific Salmon." *Freshwater Biology* 58 (2013): 1864–1877.

Laurance, William F., et al. "Ecosystem Decay of Amazonian Forest Fragments: A 22-Year Investigation." *Conservation Biology* 16 (June 2022): 605–618.

———. "The fate of Amazonian forest fragments: A 32-year investigation." *Biological Conservation* 144 (2011): 56–67.

Locke, Harvey and Wendy L. Francis. "Strategic Acquisition and Management of Small Parcels of Private Lands in Key Areas to Address Habitat Fragmentation at the Scale of the Yellowstone to Yukon Region." *Ecological Restoration* 30 (December 2012): 293–95.

Marris, Emma. "Where Peccaries Wallow, Other Animals Follow." *National Geographic.* 27 September 2014. https://www.nationalgeo graphic.com/science/article/140927-peccary-wallow-amazon-rain forest-camera-trap-biodiversity-science. Accessed 3 January 2022.

Matei, Adrienne. "What is the 'salmon cannon' and how do the fish feel about it?" *The Guardian.* 15 August 2019. https://www.theguardian .com/environment/2019/aug/15/salmon-cannon-fish-dam. Accessed 8 June 2022.

Merry, KT. "Lewa's Elephant Underpass." Render Loyalty. Website. 6 July 2017. https://www.renderloyalty.com/journal/4590/lewas-ele phant-underpass. Accessed 20 March 2022.

Miller, Matthew L. "Road Map to Refuge: As climate change forces species to move, new science is identifying habitats that—if protected— can help them survive." *Nature Conservancy* (Winter 2020): 55–59.

Min, Chew Hui and Rebecca Pazos. "Animals Crossing: Eco-Link@ BKE: Safe passage for creatures over a busy highway." *The Straits Times.* 11 December 2015. https://graphics.straitstimes.com/STI/STI-MEDIA/Interactives/2015/11/feature-ecolink-BKE-national-parks/index.html. Accessed 22 March 2022.

Pain, Stephanie. "The ant and the mandarin." *New Scientist* 170: 14 April 2001. https://www.newscientist.com/article/mg17022865-400 -the-ant-and-the-mandarin/. Accessed 1 April 2022.

Palden, Tshering. "Bhutan collars Tendrel Zangmo." *Kuensel.* 16 February 2018. https://kuenselonline.com/bhutan-collars-tendrel -zangmo/. Accessed 21 June 2022.

"The 'Path of the Pronghorn' in Wyoming." The Conservation Fund. Website. https://www.conservationfund.org/projects/the-path-of-the -pronghorn-in-wyoming. Accessed 19 March 2022.

Pratt-Bergstrom, Beth. *When Mountain Lions Are Neighbors: People and Wildlife Working It Out in California.* Berkeley, CA: Heyday, 2016.

"Problems With Big Dams." International Rivers. Website. https: //archive.internationalrivers.org/problems-with-big-dams. Accessed 7 June 2022.

"Protecting Bear Zones: Connecting Habitat (Wildlife Crossing Structures)." Parks Canada. Website. https://parks.canada.ca/pn-np /mtn/ours-bears/gestion-management/ours-bears#structures. Accessed 25 March 2022.

The Puente-Chino Hills Wildlife Corridor: Saving Urban Open Space in the Los Angeles Basin. Puente Hills Landfill Native Habitat Preservation Authority and The Trust for Public Land. 2012. https: //habitatauthority.org/newsite/wp-content/uploads/2012/04/pg1 -12v2b.pdf. Accessed 16 June 2022.

Puente Hills Habitat Preservation Authority. Website. https://www .habitatauthority.org. Accessed 16 June 2022.

Quammen, David. *The Song of the Dodo: Island Biogeography in an Age of Extinctions.* New York: Scribner, 1996.

Read, Richard. "Instead of braving the river, these endangered salmon take the highway." *Los Angeles Times.* 18 July 2021. https: //www.latimes.com/world-nation/story/2021-07-18/snake-river -salmon. Accessed 4 January 2023.

"Reducing Wildlife Vehicle Collisions by Building Crossings: General Information, Cost Effectiveness, and Case Studies from the U.S." Center for Large Landscape Conservation. Commissioned by The Pew Charitable Trust. https://www.pewtrusts.org/-/media

/assets/2020/02/reducing-wildlife-vehicle-collisions-by-build ing-crossingscllcpew-005.pdf. Accessed 1 April 2022.

Rock, Robert. "Liberty Canyon Crossing: Designing for Contextual Connectivity in the Urban Environment." Connecting People Who Connect Wildlife: Crossings, Corridors and More! Symposium at the 69th Annual Meeting of the Western Section of the Wildlife Society. 7 February 2022.

Sahagún, Louis. "Mission accomplished: Beth Pratt raised millions for a freeway overpass for L.A. cougars." *Los Angeles Times*. 11 December 2021. https://www.latimes.com/environment/story/2021-12-11 /beth-pratt-raised-millions-for-a-cougar-overpass. Accessed 27 March 2022.

——. "This architect is trying to save cougars from becoming road-kill on California freeways." *Los Angeles Times*. 4 July 2021. https:// www.latimes.com/environment/story/2021-07-04/freeway-over pass-would-save-california-cougars-from-oblivion. Accessed 26 March 2022.

Scauzillo, Steve. "Why animals are getting their own freeway over-passes in California, the West; more planned." *Whittier Daily News*. 5 July 2019. https://www.whittierdailynews.com/2019/07/05/why-an imals-are-getting-their-own-freeway-overpasses-in-california-the -west-more-planned/. Accessed 26 March 2022.

Slaght, Jonathan C.: Wildlife Biologist & Author. Website. https: //jonathanslaght.com. Accessed 11 June 2022.

Smith, Anna V. "Heartland: Reclaiming Ancestral Territory in Northern California." 24 May 2021. Trust for Public Land. Website. https://www.tpl.org/magazine/2021-spring/yurok-tribe-ancestral -homeland-kepel-california. Accessed 13 June 2022.

——. "How the Yurok Tribe is Reclaiming the Klamath River." *High Country News*. 11 June 2018. https://www.hcn.org/issues/50.10/tribal -affairs-how-the-yurok-tribe-is-reclaiming-the-klamath-river. Accessed 13 June 2022.

Smith, Heather. "Two Yurok Brothers, Four Dams, and a Lot of

Salmon" *Sierra* (September/October 2017). https://www.sierraclub .org/sierra/2017-5-september-october/act/two-yurok-brothers-four -dams-and-lot-salmon. Accessed 19 May 2022.

Soanes, Kylie and Rodney van der Ree. "Reducing road impacts on tree-dwelling animals." *Handbook of Road Ecology*. Eds. Rodney van der Ree, et al. Chichester, West Sussex: Wiley Blackwell, 2015. 334–340.

Somerville, Erin. "'Tunnel of love' below busy alpine road helping endangered pygmy possum bridge romantic divide." ABC Science News. Australian Broadcasting Corporation. 29 November 2019. https://www.abc.net.au/news/2019-11-30/tunnel-of-love-for-moun tain-pygmy-possums/11753558. Accessed 28 April 2023.

Straziuso, Jason. "How did the elephant cross the road? Underneath it." *The San Diego Union Tribune*. 28 January 2011. https://www .sandiegouniontribune.com/sdut-how-did-the-elephant-cross-the - road-underneath-it-2011jan28-story.html. Accessed 20 March 2022.

"10 quick facts about highway wildlife crossings in the park." Parks Canada: Banff National Park. Website. https://parks.canada .ca/pn-np/ab/banff/nature/conservation/transport/tch-rtc /passages-crossings

Tiger Talks: Stories of Hope from Big Cat Conservationists in Bhutan. Bhutan Foundation. Video. 29 July 2021. https://www.you tube.com/watch?v=i-gHveZdlNQ. Accessed 21 June 2022.

Tollefson, Jeff. "Splinters of the Amazon." *Nature* 496. 18 April 2013: 286–289.

van der Ree, Rodney, et al. "Wildlife Tunnel Enhances Population Viability." *Ecology & Society* 14 (2009). https://www.ecologyandsociety .org/vol14/iss2/art7/. Accessed 17 March 2022.

van der Ree, Rodney and Edgar A. van der Grift. "Recreational co-use of wildlife crossing structures." *Handbook of Road Ecology*. Eds. Rodney van der Ree, et al. Chichester, West Sussex: Wiley Blackwell, 2015. 184–189.

Vargas Soto, Juan S., et al. "Human disturbance and shifts in vertebrate community composition in a biodiversity hotspot." *Conservation Biology* 36 (2021). https://www.researchgate.net/publica tion/355209072_Human_disturbance_and_shifts_in_vertebrate _community_composition_in_a_biodiversity_hotspot. Accessed 3 March 2022.

Walker, Alissa. "World's Largest Wildlife Crossing Is Finally Under Way in Los Angeles." *Curbed*. 12 January 2022. https://www.curbed .com/2022/01/wildlife-crossing-liberty-canyon-los-angeles.html . Accessed 27 March 2022.

Waraich, Sonia. "Yurok Tribe brings 4 California condors back to the region after century-long absence." *Eureka Times-Standard*. 31 March 2022. https://www.times-standard.com/2022/03/31/yurok -tribe-brings-4-california-condors-back-to-the-region-after-century-long -absence/. Accessed 14 June 2022.

Weeks, Susie. "Case study: The Mount Kenya elephant corridor and underpass." *Handbook of Road Ecology*. Eds. Rodney van der Ree, et al. Chichester, West Sussex: Wiley Blackwell, 2015. 353–356.

Weinreb, Elaine. "A 'Way of Life at Risk': A Yurok Tribal Member's Congressional Testimony." *North Coast Journal*. 28 May 2021. https://www.northcoastjournal.com/NewsBlog/archives/2021 /05/28/a-way-of-life-at-risk-a-yurok-tribal-members-congressio nal-testimony. Accessed 18 July 2023.

Williams, J.G., et al. "Thinking like a fish: a key ingredient for development of effective fish passage facilities at river obstructions." *River Research and Applications* 28 (2012): 407–417.

Winter, Steve: Wildlife Photojournalist. Website. https://www.steve winterphoto.com/Photography/America's-Cougars/12. Accessed 4 January 2023

Young, Sansfica M. and Hiroaki Ishiga. "Environmental change of the fluvial-estuary system in relation to Arase Dam removal of the Yatsushiro tidal flat, SW Kyushu, Japan." *Environmental Earth Sciences* 72 (2014): 2301–2314.

"Zanderij Crailoo Nature Bridge." Wikipedia. https://www.wikipe.wiki /wiki/nl/Natuurbrug_Zanderij_Crailo. Accessed 24 March 2022.

Zimmerman, Barbara L. and Daniel Simberloff. "An historical interpretation of habitat use by frogs in a Central Amazonian Forest." *Journal of Biogeography* 23 (1996): 27–46.

Source Notes

Chapter 1: Home Ranges and Ranging Beyond

04 "he traveled east at least 7 miles": Sikich, Jeff. E-mail to the author. 12 January 2023.00 As they strive to create climate-wise connectivity: Anderson, unpaginated.

00 "climate-resilient" habitats: Miller, p. 58.

Chapter 2: The Problem with Patches

00 "the most important ecological experiment ever done": Tollefson, p. 286.

00 "the world's largest and longest-running experimental study of habitat fragmentation": Laurance, et al. (2011), p. 56.

00 "Of course, everybody loves a strong tiger": Beck, Harald. E-mail to the author. 15 December 2021.

00 "highly reluctant to enter clearings": Laurance, et al. (2002): p. 611.

00 to cool off or get rid of pesky parasites: Hance, Beck interview, unpaginated, and Marris, unpaginated.

00 "rather spectacular" *Phyllomedusa* tree frogs: Zimmerman, Barbara. E-mail to the author, 12 November 2021.

00 "stunned one day to find": Malcolm, Jay. E-mail to the author, 25 November 2021.

00 "the ecosystems upon which endangered species": *Endangered Species Act of 1973*, p. 1.

00 "critical habitat" zones: Ibid, p. 7.

Chapter 3: Navigating Roads of Danger

00 "which distracts birds": Khamcha, et al., unpaginated.

00 "blasts of white LED light": Rock, unpaginated.

00 "championing wildlife crossings": Lacey, Cara. Interview with the author: 31 January 2022.

Chapter 4: Reconnecting Wildlife: Underpasses, Overcrossings, and Canopy Bridges

00 In the midst of a citrus grove: Pain, unpaginated.

00 For thousands of years, citrus farmers: Ghazoul, p. 106.

00 leaf-cutting ants in Costa Rica: Farji-Brener, et al., unpaginated.

00 the first wildlife crossings in North America constructed specifically for amphibians: Mazur, Jeff. E-Mail to the author. 14 July 2023.

00 Until 1987, the first night of spring rain: "Henry Street Salamander Tunnels," unpaginated.

00 two tunnels, each approximately 28 feet (8.5 meters) long. Ibid.

00 Made from repurposed airport runway drains: Daly, unpaginated.

00 Along with habitat fragmentation: Kahn, unpaginated.

00 When the male marsupials: Ascensão, et al., p. 331

00 Thankfully, two small concrete box culverts: van der Ree, et al., unpaginated.

00 "tunnels of love": Somerville, unpaginated.

00 Though Australia's mountain pygmy possums: van der Ree, et al., unpaginated.

00 Since time immemorial, the bush elephants of this region: Weeks, pp. 353 and Straziuso, unpaginated.

00 "The elephant family groups": Weeks, Susie. E-Mail to the author. 10 March 2022.

00 Now the elephants are sharing their underpass: Ibid.

00 Moreover, anti-poaching patrols guard: Merry, unpaginated.

00 this species traces an unusually low flight pattern: Scauzillo, unpaginated.

00 As these hooved wonders: "The 'Path of the Pronghorn' in Wyoming," unpaginated.

00 "first federally protected wildlife corridor . . . United States": Hilty, et al., p. 106.

00 One notorious roadway: "Reducing Wildlife Vehicle Collisions by Building Crossings," unpaginated.

00 Here, near the capital city of Rio de Janeiro: de Souza and Lobao, unpaginated.

00 Lush with lowland Atlantic Forest: Deitz, James M.. E-mail to the author. 24 May 2023.

00 the group fought for years: Dietz, James M. E-mail to the author. 14 February 2022.

00 "provide continuous canopy over time." Dietz, James M. E-mail to the author. 24 May 2023.

00 In the meantime, crab-eating foxes. Ibid.

00 "kings of the top canopies": Erinjery, Joseph J. E-mail to the author. 23 January 2022.

00 "Sometimes they come and touch us gently": Gupta, unpaginated.

00 Los Angeles County's first dedicated wildlife underpass: Scauzillo, unpaginated.

00 this cavernous tunnel, completed in 2006: "Harbor Boulevard Wildlife Underpass," unpaginated.

Chapter 5: Safe Passage for Biodiverse Travelers: Large-Scale Wildlife Crossings

00 A series of wooden glider poles: Soanes and van der Ree, pp. 336–37 and Hall and Abson, unpaginated.

00 How do we know so much about what goes on: Abson, passim.

00 Most encouragingly, Abson discovered: Abson and Lawrence, p. 305.

00 With the Bukit Timah Reserve on one side: Min and Pazos, unpaginated.

00 cream-coloured giant squirrel and Smith's green-eyed gecko: Chen, unpaginated.

00 shaggy, nocturnal sambar deer visit the bridge: Choo, unpaginated.

00 Yet residents of Hilversum, in the Netherlands: "Zanderij Crailoo Nature Bridge," unpaginated.

00 proposed a "co-use" model: Hulzink, Poul (Senior Policy Advisor: Nature, Landscape, Recreation, and Heritage. Goois Natuurreservaat). E-Mail to the author. 23 March 2022.

00 Over one hundred eighty thousand people a year: van der Grift, Edgar A. Email to the author. 28 March 2022.

00 both creatures have recolonized: van der Grift, Edgar A. Ibid.

00 Long-term monitoring: van der Ree and van der Grift, p. 186.

00 One stretch of the Trans-Canada Highway: Kelleher, unpaginated.

00 wide-ranging grizzly bears travel: "How Did the Grizzly Bear Cross the Road?" (video).

00 scientists could watch camera-trap wildlife selfies: Ibid.

00 Though some animals, including reclusive carnivores: "10 quick facts about wildlife crossings in the park," unpaginated.

00 And mother black bears and grizzlies: "Protecting Bear Zones," unpaginated.

00 avoid the genetic disasters spawned by inbreeding: Dickie, unpaginated.

00 Covered with native foliage, these cars: Schwartz, Laurie (Public Outreach Education Officer, Banff National Park). E-Mail to the Author. 4 April 2022.

00 Canada geese, who could easily fly: Thompson, Karilynn (Promotions Officer, Parks Canada). E-Mail to the author. 18 March 2022.

Chapter 6: Bridging Traffic in Southern California: A Celebrity Mountain Lion and His Human Entourage

00 Painstakingly planting 5,000 individual plants: Rock, Robert (Principal and COO, Living Habitats). Interview with the author. 4 January 2023. Email to the author. 6 January 2023.

00 "a great ambassador for urban wildlife . . . lives up to the nickname 'ghost cat'!": Sikich, Jeff. E-Mail to the author. 29 November 2022.

00 For Pratt, these two visits were revelatory: Pratt-Bergstrom, pp. 13–22.

00 she offered a local landowner $5 for a parcel of woods: Sahagún, 27 December 2021, unpaginated.

00 "just as impacted by the roads": Pratt, Beth. E-Mail to the author. 21 March 2022.

00 "I love that this crossing . . . annual journey near and far." Ibid.

00 "have always respected . . . is very important to us": Salazar, Alan. E-Mail to the author. 4 February 2022.

00 "will provide a safe way to cross ": Ibid.

00 "wandering into extinction": Sahagún, 4 July 2021, unpaginated.

00 "we are designing for the mountain lions": Rock, Robert. E-Mail to the author. 7 March 2022.

00 "it serves our own need": Ibid.

00 "intimate and continuous . . . dry streambed": Ibid.

00 "Knitted into the adjacent landscape": Rock, unpaginated.

00 "live-in and move-through": Mariscal, Michelle. E-Mail to the author. 18 June 2021.

00 "an excellent climate-resiliency strategy": Walker, unpaginated.

Chapter 7: Down with Dams

00 "short-circuit the life cycles," "the river will have freedom to roam": Crossings Amid Climate Change (video).

00 Slope, water velocity, degree of turbulence, and access: Williams, et al., pp. 409–13.

00 a gentle, non-traumatic ride: Matei, unpaginated.

00 Finally, CalTrout is partnering: Crossings Amid Climate Change (video: Sandra Jacobson's presentation).

00: Its sequence of baffles, notches, and resting pools: Jacobson. E-Mail to the author. 19 April 2022.

00 Captured at the foot of California's Eagle Canyon: Read, unpaginated.

00 elephants, buffalos, and giraffes began "camping out": Petersen, Robin. Interviews with the author. 29 April 2022 and 16 May 2022.

00 Petersen tells me of an unusual partnership: Ibid.

00 In a big win for river restoration: Ibid.

00 But it also destroyed: Iinuma, pp.1–2.

00 the Arase trapped tons of sediment: Young and Ishiga, pp. 2301–02, 2309.

00 Villagers soon gathered: "First Dam Removal in Japan," unpaginated.

00 "symbol of true wilderness": Slaght, unpaginated.

00 They note gradual increases. Rand, Peter. E-Mail to the author. 9 May 2022.

00 finally allowing more migrating fish: Takenaka, Takeshi. E-Mail to the author. 11 May 2022.

00 Dr. Rand sees dam removal: Rand, Peter. E-Mail to the author. 9 May 2022.

00 "showy, colorful": Ibid.

00 treasuring the peninsula's entire ecosystem: Kaeriyama, Masahide. E-Mail to the Author. 18 May 2022.

00 "impede the ecological role of rivers": Ibid.

00 what ecologists call the marine-derived nutrients: Koshino, Kudo, and Kaeriyama, pp. 1864–00, 1871–74.

00 An 1855 treaty: Weinreb, unpaginated.

00 Tribal members protested: "Klamath Dam Removal Enters Home Stretch," unpaginated.

00 ancestral lifeways of the Klamath region's tribes: Smith, Anna V. (2021), unpaginated.

00 "The Indian Tribes of the [Klamath] Basin": Haaland, unpaginated.

00 "The industrial revolution is over": Smith, Heather, unpaginated.

00 "central in helping clean up": Waraich, unpaginated.

00 "We believe that he carries." Ibid.

00 The architectural ingenuity: Goldfarb, pp. 34–35.

00 "willow-log lasagna": Beesley, video.

00 "Beavers do it best": Ibid.

Chapter 8: Thinking Big: Wildlink Corridors and the Future of Connectivity

00 Conservationists, working with the California Department of Transportation: Lacey, Cara. E-Mail to the author. 25 January 2022. Principe, Zachary (Project Manager, The Nature Conservancy). E-Mail to the author. 22 February 2022.

00 Southern California's Harbor Boulevard Wildlife Underpass, *The Puente-Chino Hills Wildlife Corridor*, p. 3.

00 "toothy large carnivores": Hilty (2022), unpaginated.

00 "temperature envelope": Hilty, Jodi. E-Mail to the author. 5 May 2022.

00 Thanks to purchases, easements, and other protections: Locke and Francis, pp. 293–94.

00 "The way that wildlife sees": Hilty, Jodi. E-Mail to the author. 5 May 2022.

00 helping long-toed salamanders: Ibid.

00 Protective fencing: "Keeping toads off roads," unpaginated.

00 "continental-scale connectivity." Hilty, unpaginated.

00 When it wanders from green corridors: Cooke, pp. 60, 62–63.

00 a true mega-link: Borrell, p. 52, and Kay, unpaginated.

00 jaguars that offered some of the best clues: Vargas Soto, et al., unpaginated.

00 "Using unique spot patterns": Vargas Soto, Juan Sebastian. E-Mail to the author. 5 May 2022.

00 "Living in Harmony with Nature": *Bhutan Biological Conservation Complex* subtitle.

00 the world's first carbon sink: Gibbens, unpaginated.

00 The country's first radio-collared tiger: Palden, unpaginated.

00 "tigerscapes": Tiger Talks (video).

00 one citrus grower named Adonis: Cooke, pp. 61–62.

00 "We try to orchestrate": Molinari, Ruby. E-Mail to the author. 15 July 2021.

00 "If we are going to be farming": Ibid.

00 "new green lungs": Fuchs, unpaginated.

00 Global travelers along the East Asian-Australasian Flyway: Chen, Norah (Landscape Architect, McGregor Coxall). E-Mail to the author. 24 May 2022.

00 three prime stopover habitats: Partridge, Dustin. Interview with the author. 15 June 2022.

00 Dr. Partridge speaks fondly: Ibid.

ACKNOWLEDGMENTS

As I've traced the journeys of the remarkable creatures who populate the pages of this book, many generous guides have pointed the way. Lively emails and Zoom calls, fun field trips, perfect quotes, and even a P-22 plushie were among the cherished gifts I received from this diverse group of experts and advocates.

Within my own home range of Southern California, I want to thank Andrea Gullo (Puente Hills Habitat Preservation Authority), Gerry Hans (Friends of Griffith Park), Jennifer Hoffman (Western Riverside County Multiple Species Habitat Conservation Plan), Megan Jennings (San Diego State University), and Travis Martz (Santiago Oaks Regional Park) for responding quickly and graciously to my emails. Sandra Jacobson of CalTrout helped me better understand aquatic connectivity while Trish Smith and Zachary Principe of The Nature Conservancy shared invaluable information about local crossings and corridors projects.

In Amherst, Massachusetts, Jeff Mazur of the Hitchcock Center for the Environment helped me appreciate the ingenuity (and charm!) of the Henry Street Salamander Tunnels.

Along the forested streambanks of Northern California, Kyle Achziger and Sarah Beesley explained how indigenous species of the coast redwoods region find connectivity over land and through water.

Three illustrious scientists long involved in the Biological Dynamics of Forest Fragments Project (BDFFP) provided detailed and eloquent answers to my questions about this incredible, ongoing experiment in the Amazon rainforest. Thank you, William Laurance, Jay Malcolm, and Barbara Zimmerman!

Adrián Munguia Vega and Elizabeth Dávalos-Dehullu helped me understand key concepts related to habitat fragmentation.

Virginia Delgas, Karilynn Thompson, and especially Laurie

Schwartz of Parks Canada offered a wealth of information about the world-famous system of wildlife crossings in Banff National Park.

Researching the Yellowstone to Yukon Conservation Initiative (Y2Y), I was very lucky indeed to connect with Mark Hebblewhite and Kelly Zenkewich. !

In the Netherlands, Poul Hulzink and Edgar van der Grift offered vivid descriptions of flora and fauna that made the Natuurbrug Zanderij Crailoo, truly come alive for me.

Bio-technician Jacques Venter of Kruger National Park patiently and precisely answered technical questions about the dams that dot this jewel of South Africa.

I send thanks to James Conroy, Sunny Zhu, and especially Norah Chen for teaching me about the Lingang Bird Sanctuary.

Three experts on the rivers of Shiretoko National Park in Hokkaido, Japan helped me grasp how the removal of dams can help salmonid species, as well as other wildlife in the region. I'm grateful to Masahide Kaeriyama, Peter Rand, and Takeshi Takenaka, the latter of whom joined forces with Jonathan C. Slaght to make me fall in love with the Blakiston's fish owl.

Scientists and advocates around the world shared their expertise on, and genuine affection for, the captivating coaltion of species that moves through the pages of this book: Susie Weeks (Kenya's African elephants), Juan Sebastián Vargas Soto (Baird's tapirs of Costa Rica), James M. Dietz (Brazil's golden lion tamarins), Joseph J. Erinjery and Trisha Gupta (India's lion-tailed macaques), and Hayley Bates and Dean Heinze (Australia's mountain pygmy possums). Abundant thanks to you all.

The following individuals each deserve a separate acknowledgments section.

With his profound knowledge and infectious enthusiasm, Harald Beck, tropical ecologist and cochair of the IUCN SSC Peccary Specialist Group, introduced me to the inimitable white-lipped peccary.

Cara Lacey of The Nature Conservancy and Jodi Hilty of the

Yellowstone to Yukon Conservation Initiative taught me that thinking big while cherishing small victories is the way to go.

Robin Petersen, Kruger National Park's aquatic biologist extraordinaire, met me several times on Zoom across time zones, sent me troves of invaluable matérials, and brought me on board Team African Eel.

Dustin Partridge of NYC Audubon evocatively described the rich assemblage of pollinator pathways and bird stopover sites in the city.

Two memorable field trips inestimably enriched my research. Ruby Molinari and Lucas Carlow gave me a wonderfully up-close look at Apricot Lane Farms in Moorpark, California. A month later, I spent an unforgettable morning at the Puente Hills Habitat Preserve with Michelle Mariscal. Thank you for these excursions.

The Wallis Annenberg Wildlife Crossing team is at the very center of the connectivity story told here: Jeff Sikich of the National Parks Service, Robert Rock of Living Habitats, Chumash and Tataviam tribal elder Alan Salazar, Korinna Domingo of the Cougar Conservancy, Katharine Pakradouni of the Santa Monica Mountains Fund, and especially Beth Pratt of the National Wildlife Federation and #SaveLACougars. Thank you all so very much.

P-22 (2010–2022): you are the true spirit of this book. Long Live the King.

The paw prints and hoofprints of four treasured animal companions—Benjamin, Mischa, Zodiac, and Apollo—secretly stamp every page here.

To Della Farrell, my incredible editor at Holiday House, I offer profound thanks for your expertise and enthusiasm. A shared love of words and of the natural world has made for a truly special partnership. I'm also grateful for the expertise and support of the whole Holiday House team, including Kerry Martin, Emily Stone, and Emma Swan. Thank you, Jamie Green, for bringing the book's themes and scenes to life with your exquisite illustrations.

A huge thank you to my wonderful colleagues, also close friends, at the University of California, Los Angeles: Bruce Beiderwell, Leigh Harris, Christine Holten, Janette Lewis, Michele Moe, Shelby Popham, Bruce Stone, Daniel Sussman (who also took my author photo), and Jennifer Westbay. Jennifer Westbay. I'm grateful to UCLA Research and Instruction Librarian Sylvia Page.

Another circle of friends, some of them lifelong: Ed Frankel, Julie Giese, Suzanne Greenberg, Dorian Johnson, Jodi Johnson, Isha Anish Khanzode, Kathleen Lundeen, Frank Martinelli, Jennie Kearl Welsh, and Nick Welsh for your abiding friendship. And for her steadfast support, both practical and spiritual, I want to thank Amy Dehnert with all my heart. .

Finally, my family has given me love, companionship, and needed respites throughout this project. I'm grateful for my amazing sister, Lauri Rowland; my brother-in-law, Mitch Rowland; my aunt (and very dear friend), Mary Standlee; my all-time favorite uncle, Don Standlee; and my cousin and cherished friend, Brent Standlee. My sons, Alexey Gabriel Bonca and Nicolai Adrian Bonca: you are the very heart of my life, and my most treasured readers. Thank you for hiking, camping, watching wildlife (elk in the redwoods!), and simply sharing your lives with me.

To my mother, Nadine Chichester, and in loving memory of my father, Ben Chichester, I dedicate this book. Some of my earliest recollections take me back to Prairie Creek Redwoods State Park, where my father was a Park Interpreter, a gifted naturalist and professor of botany who shared with campground visitors, and with his family, his love of the big trees, lush ferns, and all the native wildlife (including banana slugs, for whom my mom penned a catchy ditty!). My parents planted the seed for this book, and I thank them both for teaching me to feel at home in the natural world. It's a home, a habitat that we share with the world's wild creatures, and it's our task, and our honor, to protect it.

INDEX

TK 4 PAGES

[INDEX]